Practical Steelhead Fishing

PRACTICAL STEELHEAD FISHING

by Jim Freeman

SOUTH BRUNSWICK
NEW YORK: A. S. BARNES and CO., INC.
LONDON: THOMAS YOSELOFF LTD

Library of Congress Catalogue Number: 66-13767

A. S. Barnes and Co., Inc.
South Brunswick, New Jersey

Thomas Yoseloff Ltd
18 Charing Cross Road
London W.C. 2, England

6414

Printed in the United States of America

To Patsy, who was always there

Contents

Illustrations

Practical Steelhead Fishing

1 Meeting the Steelhead

The steelhead is one fish that lives up to his reputation. He will fight harder, run longer, jump more frequently and will be bigger than any other trout. To top off his fine array of talents, the steelie is the most beautiful of all the trouts in sheer piscatorial good looks. And every angler who has read of him or talked to the enthusiast who has tangled with this smart aleck from salt water wants to take a crack at fishing for him.

But it is indeed a rare and lucky man who merely hefts his rod and goes out to knock over a steelhead the first time. In fact, the common idea among most steelheaders with experience at this game is that the beginning angler will be lucky to feel the power of a good steelie before he's had at least two years to learn the trade. But I don't think it is necessary for the beginner to spend even a full season before he gets going as a steelheader!

If the angler will start out right and follow a few of the rules that all steelheaders have to know, there is no reason why he can't get into a run and then to catch fish before the kinks are stretched out of his newest coil of line.

The essential thing that an angler has to conquer is a basic knowledge of the type of fish he's dealing with. Throughout this book there will be sprinklings of steelheading lore that can add to both the pleasure and background of the steelhead man. But here we'll give a thumbnail sketch of a steelhead's life cycle.

To begin with, a steelhead is nothing more—and nothing less—than a rainbow trout. The scientific name of both fish is *salmo gairdneri*. The thing that gives the steelhead his strength and class is the fact that he has gone off to sea, the Pacific Ocean. The scientists call any fish who spends part of his time in salt water, and part in fresh water, an anadromous species. But, from the angler's point of view, the charming thing about this setup is that the steelie comes back with twice the strength and several times the size of any brother rainbow who remained by the fireside in the stream.

Life starts for the steelhead down under the gravel of some stream that flows into the Pacific Ocean somewhere between Mexico and Alaska. To be more exact, the city of Monterey in central California is normally considered the southern limit of the steelies' range, and the Aleutian Islands in Alaska is considered as the northern limit. There are a few minor runs of fish in streams down into Mexican waters, and recently there have been some Russian experiments with salmons and steelheads from Siberia to the coast of Norway, but these are of small interest to the average angler.

Anyway, our fighting steelhead gets his first grip on life as a tiny fellow buried from 6 in. to 18 in. under the bottom of the stream. At this stage of the game he's a pretty ugly looking affair, not much more than an indication of a head and tail sticking out from either end of a ¼ inch egg. But it's not his fault that his beautiful mother stuffed him there along with a few thousand of his brothers and sisters from a few weeks to a few months ago. One nice thing about being tucked down there under the rocks is that he's as safe from hungry predators as he'll ever be for the rest of his life. The only thing that can knock him off at this time is some form of suffocation, such as a lumber operation upstream from the spawning beds that lets silt settle into the cracks between the rocks and gravel; or perhaps a new industry that discharges a type of waste into the stream that takes the oxygen out of the water; or a new city that dumps its sewage into the stream; or some of the new farm fertilizers that have the unhappy attribute of draining nitrates into the stream; or . . . But we can save this for a later chapter.

The tiny steelhead eventually wriggles out through the cracks in the gravel and rocks and starts his life as a full-fledged swimming creature. About this same time, he gets rid of his ugly egg sac and starts to look somewhat like a fish, though he's a bit stubby and his swimming leavse a lot to be desired. It is at this stage, and for the next year or so, that the young parr or fingerling steelhead lives a life more perilous than any TV hero. From his first peek out of the stones, just about everything from bugs and birds to frogs and bigger fish try their best to assassinate him. But if he's nimble, he dodges long enough and is able to do in his own share of smaller creatures. Usually by the time the following spring rolls around the little steelie is from 6 in. to 9 in. long and he decides to sidestep the whole matter of existence in this perilous habitat and he starts drifting off downstream.

Young steelheads do not merely turn around and swim downstream at the end of their second year in the stream. They continue to face the current and sort of back into their new life. This trip can take anywhere from a few weeks to many months, depending on what stage of growth they decide to make the descent downstream, and just how far upstream they were when they got the urge to move. At this stage they are faced with new dangers. They are ravenous feeders and they travel in groups of a few fish to huge shoals; pint-sized versions of their parents. Any angler who wants to can stand in just about any good riffle and yank these little tykes out by the hundreds. If the path of the stream goes through farm or range land there's a good chance that thousands—if not millions—of these baby steelheads will follow their adventurous natures and get sidetracked or lost in the miles of irrigation ditches and canals that this kind of real estate features. But this last peril is being slowly conquered by putting up screens to keep the little travellers from being sucked up by pumps or diverted by these side channels. Eventually, the remaining fish reach the tidal stretch of their natal river.

In the tidewater, the tiny steelhead pauses for a few days or weeks to get a new grip on life. Here they finally find the big treat of salt water—abundant food. They fool around for a while in this brackish water and most of them simply turn away from the current of the river and dive right into the deeps of the Pacific. Exactly where they go during this first foray into the salt is their own secret. However, it is probable that they merely drop off the continental shelf into deep water where they take up a life of peace and plenty.

A percentage of the fish that enter salt water as youngsters, 6 to 9 in. long, either like the life in the tide pools and the salt water near the mouths of the river, or they feel the urge to go back upstream for reasons of their own. And once the fish are in salt water they break up into separate groups. The majority of these fish that have been successful in reaching salt water will spend approximately two years at the big dining table of the sea. But a percentage of them do not conform to this rule. They return to their natal rivers at different times.

In order to tell the difference between the biggest steelheads and these splinter groups, fishermen have devised a novel way of name tagging them. This naming corresponds to the size of the fish being taken at any time of the year and sometimes to the season. In some areas, the fish which come into fresh water are called "bluebacks." Why this is necessary, nobody has ever quite explained satisfactorily. The best guess on this subject is that when they have blue dividing lines between their backs and their silver stomachs, they have definitely been in salt water for some time. Whereas, the small estuary fish are still trout colored, much the same as the rainbow members of the tribe.

But in most areas throughout the steelhead's range, the anglers have let this matter of fish color go. Instead they have come to call any fish that weighs less than three pounds on the scales a "half-pounder." Again, the logic of calling a fish that can weigh up to three pounds a half-pounder is difficult to figure out. But, for our purposes here, we'll stick to the tradition and call them half-pounders.

These migrating fish of smaller size are primarily important to the serious steelhead fisherman because they are the basic fish in the streams during the summer and fall months. Streams such as the Eel and Klamath in California; the Kalama, Washougal, Wind in Washington; the Rogue and Umpqua in Oregon; and virtually all of the streams in British Columbia, are noted for these summer and fall run fish. Also, these fish appeal to the fishermen primarily interested in fly fishing because these rivers are at their smallest flow at this time of year.

Of course, at this same time of year there are a number of larger fish that will go considerably over the three pound mark, and fishermen who work these summer streams consider them really choice items in their creel. And there seems to be a fairly well worked out plan to these things.

The Pacific salmons, which use the same streams as the steelheads, have this same basic pattern of life. A percentage of the fish will return as so called "chubs," which correspond to the half-pounder steelhead runs. Virtually 100 per cent of these chubs are male fish and they precede the runs of fully matured fish. It seems to be nature's plan to provide these additional males to make certain that all of the successfully nested eggs of the all important female fish get an adequate chance at being fertilized. And this way, if some kind of catastrophe should threaten the existence of the species, there is already a built in edge against their being annihilated.

This built in safety factor extends even back to the important spawning grounds. Approximately 60 per cent of the steelheads migrate to the sea during the spring months at the age of two years. Roughly 35 per cent of the fish stay for a full three years before they decide to migrate. And as a safety factor a few maverick fish never do migrate to salt water; rather, they remain in fresh water and develop into the common rainbow trout, so dear to the trout fisherman's heart.

The important thing the beginner at this steelheading game should realize is that every stream that has a good run of half-pounders and early fish has a much better and bigger run of large, winter run fish at a different time of the year. These real migrations of big fish normally start sometime in November and continue through the month of February in most streams. For the time being, we'll leave this subject, but it's well that the beginner keep this bit of information tucked away on the top of his head.

Now, back to those wise fish that have taken the straight and narrow path of the average steelhead and have dropped off the continental shelf. They were two years old when they took the plunge. And they were from 6 in. to 9 in. in length. We don't see them for about two years. Some specimens even soak up the good living for as much as five years, although they are very rare individuals, and two to three years would be an average time for them to spend in salt water. When we next catch sight of them, they are something to warm the heart of a fishing man.

The once little fish are now in a class by themselves, and they go from about 20 in. to 36 in. in length. And they will pull the scales down from 6 lbs. to a tops of maybe 30 lbs., which is a lip-smacking size for any trout. It is also a fine endorsement for the food supply in salt water when you consider that a couple of years in fresh water barely gets the fish big enough to swim for themselves, and the same amount of time out in the salt has made them top dog when they come back home to go through their spawning rites. It is at this point in their lives, when they reach the mouth of their natal stream, that the interest of the angling public reaches a white hot pitch.

The average winter run fish will go around 8 lbs., a handy size. But it is not size alone that distinguishes them from other trouts. When the angler meets them under the proper conditions, in the lower stretches of the rivers, they are at their fighting best. They are strong and charged with a peculiar energy that is both nervous and fierce. The first fish in the winter runs in most rivers are still feeding fairly well because their roe or milt sacs are not bloated or enlarged. These fish, normally taken from late October to the end of November in most years, are at the absolute top of the piscatorial ladder. They have the weight and size to go the limit, and if they are taken in the lower stretches of most rivers, they will virtually fight to the end of their lives. It's a thrill worth waiting a lifetime for.

As the winter months go by the fish become more and more anxious to get their spawning duties over with. As soon as a few good winter storms open the riffles upstream they hustle right along, rarely pausing for more than a brief rest. And this is when the angler has to be on his toes. In fact, an experienced steelhead man knows that the real secret of catching steelheads is more a matter of finding where they are at any given time than it is a matter of some secret lure or bait, once the run is actually located.

A good deal of this book will be devoted to the art of locating a run of fish, then of using the right kind of tackle and auxiliary equipment to put the angler into them. But right now, let's start weaning the angler, who cut his teeth on other species, to some of the mistakes that we've seen trout or bass anglers make over the last 20 years.

It sounds simple enough to merely say that the steelheads are a migrating, moving population of fish. But trying to cure an angler who has spent his entire angling career in trout streams trying to find solitude is something else. In the first place, the trout-trained man dreams of finding a long stretch of good water where his fellow anglers haven't gotten in before him and beat the water to a froth. He will pack in almost any distance and suffer almost any hardship to get at virgin waters. If he works hard at getting off the beaten track, he will, eventually, be rewarded with good or excellent catches of fish.

Steelheading doesn't work this way! I'll repeat that for emphasis: *Steelheading does not work this way!*

Virtually every single steelhead stream—and there are hundreds of them on the Pacific slope—in the continental United States, that amounts to anything, from the average angler's point of view, has a road running right beside it. And the fishing is just as likely to be terrific 50 feet from the paved road as it is 50 miles back in the bush.

It is absolutely essential that the beginner understand this point because far too many have become discouraged when they've seen a line-up of steelhead fishermen at a spot where they've been told by some knowledgeable friend that the fishing was good. In fact, if the beginner goes to a stretch of river and finds that he has it all to himself, it's a pretty good indication that he is fishing in water that doesn't hold any fish at that particular time. The reason for this "follow-the-crowd" approach to the game is that most of the local talent will know as soon as a run of fish enters any of the streams. So, it's a pretty rare day when a beginner can stumble across a run of fish that has missed the attention of the anglers who have been fishing these same waters for many years.

Another item that the beginner should put in his pipe is the fact that there is no such thing as a good or a bad steelhead stream. Any stream can be good to an angler who manages to get there when the fish are in and hitting. So, just because a stream is world famous, as is the Klamath or Rogue or Kispiox, doesn't necessarily mean that it will be good to any angler who doesn't manage to get on the water when the fish are in it.

It seems strange to me, but I've run into this item of prejudice against the crowds in hundreds of beginning anglers; and in many experienced anglers who should know better by now. I have stood in, around, and across streams from hundreds of steelhead line-ups. And the only thing I've been able to tell for sure about every last one of them is that the same few anglers—usually less than one in ten of them—took the majority of fish yesterday, are taking the majority of fish today, and if you come back tomorrow, you'll find that they are still taking the majority of fish then. In short, the steelhead fisherman is a rare animal, but the people who go steelhead fishing are legion.

Later in this work we will give specific tips and complete programs for the techniques of how to find a run of fish, then on how to take the fish that are available. Usually it's merely a matter of having the right equipment with you on the stream and knowing how to do the right thing with that equipment. I have found that there is very little difference between the guy who consistently takes fish and the one who habitually goes home with light stringers or no fish at all.

As long as we're on the subject of techniques I'd like to mention that there is no single piece of equipment or type of fishing gear that will work under all of the many hundreds of conditions that the steelhead angler will run into. The rivers into which steelheads run range all the way from tiny creeks to raging monsters. If the angler insists on taking his fish in only one specific way, he'll meet his comeuppance in a hurry, and the steelheads will end up with the last laugh by dying of old age rather than crossing the palate of the appreciative angler.

To sew up a few loose ends concerning the steelhead's destiny on his spawning run: the runs of fish proceed upstream at different rates of travel in different streams. The time of year that they enter the stream, the individual condition of different fish, and the type of water that they swim in are all important factors in the life of the steelhead. But the most important single item that controls their travels and the fishing habits of the anglers is the weather. The Pacific slope is normally a rain forest area. Snow, except in the extreme northern end of the range, is rare; but the angler should expect to do a good bit of rainy weather fishing. Without the rain it's doubtful that the fish would be moving or hitting.

As the steelheads get closer to their spawning grounds, they start to lose a good deal of their willingness to strike, and they are drained of some of their spawning power that was so noteworthy when they were in the lower stretches of the stream. It's a common thing nowadays for the fish and game departments to put this spawning area off limits to fishing. This is a good thing and it will probably become more evident as the years roll past.

There are techniques that will let the angler get into this great trout at any stage of his life cycle, with the exception of his salt water sojourn. We'll cover them step by step. . . .

2 Riggings for Steelheads

There is a great welter of equipment on the shelves in most tackle stores. In the west, a great percentage of it masquerades under the heading of "steelhead tackle." Some of it is steelhead gear of the highest order. Some of it is junk, pure and simple.

To start with, just about every known type and size of fishing equipment, from rods to reels and even the lures and baits that are available at all, have at one time or another taken some steelheads. Taking baits as a simple example, I once talked to a salty old Klamath River fly purist who was over seventy years old. He'd been scragging his share of steelies for almost 50 years, and when I met him he was still quite a man with these great fish. The old boy put it this way, "This season," he said (it was the 1961 season), "every damned fisherman on the river is using worms, most of 'em think night crawlers are th' only thing. I've seen fresh roe have its day. I've seen the Flatfish come and go, the yarn flies, the Cherry Bobber, the Spin-N-Glo, the Wobble-Rite and the Mepps've all had their day. Why son, if everyone was usin' shoe horns, then shoe horns would be ketchin' all the fish, and they'd be the famous bait. . . ."

The old gentleman had a point. A great deal of the success element with any lure, bait, or type of equipment simply depends on the length of time it is kept in the water. And if the type of bait or lure used is kept in the right place in the water, we have the makings of a fish killing setup. The unfortunate part of this is that the angler doesn't actually have very much to say about the type of equipment he will use for his steelheading. The situation, that is, the fishing conditions under which he has to fish, actually dictates the type of gear that has any chance at all.

This does not mean, by any means, that an individual angler cannot insist that his fish be taken with a certain kind of tackle. But it does mean that he will be forced to go out and find a set of conditions under which he can use that particular equipment. For instance, the fly fisherman has to realize that he cannot operate on many of the weed-choked and brushy banked streams that are characteristic of most of the tiny streams that hold some real populations of fish. Or, a man who insists that he take his steelheads with a small ultra-light spin outfit is almost hopelessly undergunned in the tidal stretches of virtually every river or creek—the prime spot to do battle with the steelie. But what the average beginner at this game is interested in is a single outfit that will do a good job under the majority of conditions he's likely to find. Is there such an outfit?

I think so! But to explain why I feel the angler should consider the merits of this particular outfit, I'd like to explain my reasons a bit.

I have fished in most of the major steelhead waters in the continental U.S. Most of my experience has been in the southern end of the range, in California waters, but I've seen enough of the tackle used throughout the range to make a good estimate of what the boys use in the other parts of this steelhead territory. Actually, the basic gear will change from one river to the next, no matter where in the range the fisherman is working. For instance, a big, wide river will demand big, long range tackle. But this same long rod is a torture to snake through the brambles of a brushy stream; hence, small streams breed small fishing poles, and big streams demand long rods. So for the sake of convenience I've chosen the line strength element as the determining factor.

Steelheads cause fishermen to become lyrical after the fish are caught, eaten, and gone. In short, their memory grows with age, like fine wine or a departed love. A man who through experience has come to habitually use 10 lb. test monofilament tippets on his fly rod in actual fishing may, with the use of "anglers license" and faulty memory, shave that tippet size down to perhaps 6 lbs. for the sake of a barroom discussion or a plain old fireside tale. But when using the newer monofilaments on the market and considering the steelhead under the average fishing and water conditions, a 10 lb. test hunk of monofilament is a pretty good choice for a starter. So without considering any other element but the fish himself, a man using 10 lb. line would be in pretty good shape, regardless of what *type* of gear he is using to take his steelheads.

However, there is much more to this steelheading game than merely landing a fish once he's hooked. One of the biggest chores of the steelhead fisherman, on just about any stream, is water coverage. And water coverage means a long rod.

Throughout the range of the steelheads, fishermen have settled on one particular size rod to get this job done. It's true that in some locations, such as on the central Oregon coastal streams, these rods tend to have a bit more beef in them than they do in others; and in other areas, such as the tributary streams that flow into the Columbia River from both the Washington and Oregon side, as well as the average California streams, these rods tend to be on the light side. But there is one length of rod that is almost universal in steelhead among the experienced talent—it's 9 ft.

This may seem the long way around merely saying that the angler is better off with a 9 ft. rod than any other, but as I pointed out, there is a lot of gear that masquerades under the title of steelhead equipment.

These 9 ft. steelhead rods—it's the same with any of the three basic fishing methods, fly, spin, or level wind gear—have evolved over a period of many years. They are the product of millions of hours of fishing, thought, and design. The beginner or newcomer to this game is more than likely travelling a well-worn path if he finds himself experimenting with a rod that's very far from this length.

We'll leave the discussion of fly rod outfits to a separate chapter and just concentrate on the two other types of gear: spin and level wind. All types and sizes of rigs have their place in steelheading, but as soon as the angler visits any steelhead stream I am certain that he will see nine out of ten anglers using spinning equipment. And almost that many will be using 9 ft. rods that are rather stiff.

The next thing that he will see is that most of the anglers are using standard fresh water—open face—spinning reels with line that tests from 10 lbs. to 15 lbs. There are literally hundreds of thousands of these outfits in action on our steelhead streams, and it's rare when that many working fishermen are wrong! I would say that the angler should stick to the standard (fresh water) spinning reels, although this is not an essential point.

The fresh water models of most standard make spinning reels, such as the Mitchell 300 or the Quick Junior, will hold enough line in the 10 lb. to 15 lb. test class to handle all but the rare steelhead. They also have the additional advantage of being well known and well distributed, so that standard parts can be found in any medium or large sized city. Too, they are light, compact, and fit any rod of the type we recommend here. The exact brand name doesn't make much difference, just as long as the quality is good—essential in steelheading because this fish will strain even good tackle—and that the brand name is a popular one. I definitely suggest that the angler avoid using any of the "enclosed spool" reels for general steelheading. They have a very definite place in steelheading, but we'll take this up later.

So, to sum up thus far: We have suggested a 9 ft. rod, fitted with a standard model, open face spinning reel and loaded with line that tests between 10 lbs. and 15 lbs. This outfit will let an angler catch more fish under more situations than any other I know and with less trouble.

To add a bit of selectivity to this outfit, it's a good idea to invest in a couple of extra spools of line to fit the reel chosen. There are times in steelhead fishing when the angler will want to use light weights and still cast for respectable distances. If he only has one size line, say the 15 lb. test on a single spool, he'll either find it impossible to sling light weights for any appreciable distance or it will be so irksome to get the job done that he'll lose a good deal of the fun of the game. If the angler is strapped for money, I'd say that he should at least buy a spool filled correctly with 8 lb. test line and another filled correctly with 15 lb. test line. (In every case, of course, the line should be good quality monofilament nylon. Cheap line is a waste of money in any case.) And it is more important to keep these spools filled to the correct place on the spool with fresh line—line should be replaced at least twice a season—than it is to have 20 different spools with checked line or incorrectly loaded onto the spool.

As soon as finances allow, the angler should try to get hold of spools of line that go from 6 lb. test to 18 lb. test. In my own spinning set I have six separate spools on any trip, and I usually carry several of them with me when I am actually on the stream fishing—I'll explain why later. These spools of line are important in this order: 8 lb., 15 lb., 12 lb., 10 lb., 18 lb. and 6 lb. And this is the order in which they should be purchased if the angler is serious about doing a good job under the conditions he'll find.

I find myself using the 8 lb. spool and the 12 lb. spool more often than any other, so I always carry a couple hundred yards of extra line this size on any trip I make. Another item I've found important is to make sure that I have each spool loaded with exactly 100 yds. of line, regardless of the size on any given spool. This takes a good deal of manipulation, but it's worth the trouble to make sure that the spool is filled to within $1/8$ inch of the spool lip when you get done winding on exactly 100 yds. Actually, the first time I wind on the line I usually have to go through the whole operation from two to five times to accomplish this. But once it's done, it's done for good and I can get rid of a bunch of frayed nylon monofilament when I'm actually out fishing in only a few minutes. Take my word for it, it's worth the added trouble.

When selecting any rod for steelhead fishing the angler is stuck with the inexact job of guessing how that particular rod will actually operate once it's in action. And the anglers I've seen in a tackle store buying a rod all go through the same procedure: They finger the various rods first; they finally choose a model that catches their eye; they find an open space, usually in some aisle; and they switch the rod back and forth. They are accomplishing exactly nothing. Even a man with many years of rod building experience cannot tell anything from merely switching a rod back and forth. But who can resist this venerable pastime; it's standard procedure, much like kicking the tires of cars on a used car lot while you're making up your mind about the deal. But, there is one simple test that the angler can go through if he wants to check on a rod before he buys it.

First of all, choose a couple of good looking rods from the rack in the 9 ft. class. (One of the best ways that the angler can decide which of the rods available are worth consideration is to look at the metal fittings. I've never seen a good rod fitted with bad metal; I've never seen a poor rod with good metal!) Next, have a clerk hold the butt end of the rod flush with a counter, and let the rod extend out into an aisle or any convenient open space. Then, get a snap swivel for each rod and an 8 oz. weight from the lead counter in the store. Attach the lead weight to the tip top of the rods with the snap swivel and let them droop down as far as they'll go. Now, merely step to one side and sight along the side view of the rods to see exactly where they bend. You'll probably have to squat and do a good deal of pondering.

This is known, in engineering circles, as "establishing a static bend," but the practical application is that the angler can now make an intelligent selection, at least from among the two or three rods that he has available to him in that particular store. What the angler is looking for is a progressive bend in a steelhead rod—actually, every properly designed rod for fishing of any kind should have this progressive bend. The bulk of the bending should be

more or less evenly distributed throughout the full length
of the rod. If the tip droops too much or too much of the
bend comes in the butt section, the angler will have a rod
that will either whiplash in the tip or will lack built-in
strength for decent casting. It's surprising how many good
quality makes of rods have defects of this kind in them.
Anyway, this procedure is interesting to go through, and
it will give the angler some indication of how powerful
the different rods actually are. About the best indication
of a rod with power is the spot where the weights end up.
The one farthest from the floor is the most powerful of the
selection being tested.

The rods I personally use are those that do a good all-
around job for me. I have a new Fenwick FS 90 that feels
very soft in the hands but has surprising power when it's
put into action. The rod I used for several years was one
that I made up myself from a Lima Glas 1145 blank, and
it had a much faster, stiffer action than any other of com-
parable weight that I have tried. I own a Garcia 2651
(Conolon) rod that has seen a lot of service. This is an
8½ ft. rod with a lot of power. A Harnell 865 and Harnell
630 do fair work, especially in tidal waters, but I use them
with a larger reel.

I am not slavish in my own use of rods. I prefer the
smallest, lightest rod that will get the particular job I
want done for me. I have even used a 10 ft. Harnell 675R
where extreme casts are necessary. But I do not like to
hold a rod this big up in the air for a whole day on a steelhead stream. However, it will give fantastic distances to
2 oz. weights when the big reels that fit it are loaded with
line of about 12 lb. test.

When the reader looks over the selection in a tackle
store he should try to decide on a rod that will bend well
down into the butt section for his first basic rod. These
rods, in modern day selections offered by most com-

panies, invariably turn out to be the most pleasant to use over a period of time. The softness of the butt section may not feel as nice as the peppy, stiff rods, but with a bit of experience, the angler will come to like them once they are in action. Too, they resist the strong spurts in the run of a typical steelhead better than a stiff-butt rod. One important item for the angler to remember is that the butt, from reel seat to the back end of the butt, should definitely measure at least 12 in. This length is exactly right so that the rod can be tucked under the elbow to ease the strain on a wrist through long hours of casting and drift fishing.

So far I haven't mentioned the modern level wind reels and rods that are becoming the rage of the steelhead waters since the early fifties. The main reason that I do not consider these outfits as practical for the average steelhead fisherman as the common spinning rig is that they are much more expensive to set up in the first place, and they are far harder to learn to use with any degree of adeptness.

Actually, before World War II, the dedicated steelhead fisherman who fished at all was stuck with level wind gear for his heavy duty winter steelhead fishing, even if he was devoted to the single other method then available—fly fishing. Most of these old timers have never even considered changing over to the more adaptable spin gear, and they have gone on using their pet level wind reels and rods throughout the years since spinning became such a world beater. But anyone who has had experience with these level wind setups knows that they can only do certain jobs perfectly. Many of the chores expected of good steelhead gear can't be done at all with any level wind rod and reel.

The main reason that level wind gear of any kind is not

as adaptable as spinning equipment is the need to use heavier weights to get the same distances. And, while the solution is simply to add a few grains of lead to the casting end of the rig, these few grains can spell the difference between success and failure in much—if not the majority —of steelheading success. And, no matter how you figure it, the angler using a level wind reel has to have this extra weight because he has to get the spool of the level wind revolving.

It is really a pleasure for me to watch a good level wind man in operation—usually an older man with many years of experience. But I have had many years of this kind of casting myself and I can admit to the limitations of this kind of gear. There is one job that the level wind outfit will do better than any other—it will cast to much longer ranges than any other kind of tackle.

In steelhead country a level wind outfit is commonly called a "meat rod." And this is a pretty good indication of its chore in this game. Whenever the dedicated steelheader finds himself faced with the job of making ultralong casts to get at fish that perenially lay over on the other side of the river or lagoon, he turns to his pet level wind gear to get the job done. This is what I use my own level wind equipment for.

My own tackle rack has three level wind rigs that have taken me many hours and years of experiment to set up. They range from 9 ft. to 11 ft. in length and I had more trouble matching up the rod length, line strength, and reel models to them than I had with all my other fishing equipment combined. The reason is that when you are reaching out for those maximum distance casts, that the level winders do so well, everything becomes critical. Everything has to work smoothly or I spend most of my fishing time fighting with the equipment rather than fighting fish. One of the most important elements in this extreme distance casting is the angler himself. I find that on some days—especially those very cold mornings when my fingers are near the freezing point—I cannot thumb the spool of the reel with enough finesse to do any kind of good job with my distance rigs. But, this does add to the charm of this level winding game.

The heart of level wind gear is the reel. Here there is very little room for choice by the angler. Good level wind reels are a masterpiece of engineering and workmanship. And they cost real money. Most of the reels that are worth considering at all are priced at $40 or more; so you can't afford to make many mistakes when you choose them. Next, you've got to choose a line that will give you good service and match the whole works up with a rod that is exactly right, giving the proper backbone for distance casting and yet being sensitive enough in the tip section so you can do a talented job of feeling out the bottom.

I know of no way to tell an individual angler how to choose and use a level wind outfit. The reason is that there is so much of the human element involved in thumbing the reel spool. I've repeatedly seen one angler pick up a specific level wind rig and manage to get extreme distance into his casts. Then another angler will pick up the same exact rod and make a bird's nest that's something to write home about. However, I can give the rods and reels that I have personally used with success, and the reader can then choose for himself. Of course, any selection of tackle is an intensely personal matter for any serious angler so I don't insist that the outfits I personally use are the absolute best in any category.

The first rig is built around the Pflueger Supreme reel; the older models that have been standards for many years. I use this reel with a Harnell 625R rod, which for me bends well down into the butt on the cast and gives the necessary slow start to the heavier reel spool on the Supreme.

With an Ambassadeur 6000 I can get fine casts from this same Harnell 625R rod, with the spool loaded with 15 lb. test line and all of the counter weights removed, just as long as I keep the reel well oiled. In this kind of casting it is essential that the reel be kept in top shape and that the pawl be changed at least once every season. I have used monofilament line for all of my level wind casting for the last several years and I have had some monumental snarls—where the cure is to cut the line away with a knife or scissors if I goof.

I use an Ambassadeur 5000 on a rod made up on the same Lima Glas 1145 rod blank for the majority of my own level wind fishing. This reel fitted with 12 lb. test monofilament from one of the "limp" brands is a joy to use, and it will do just about anything that could be asked of a level wind outfit. I've used this reel with the Harnell 625R and it does an adequate job for me. But the Lima Glas rod has been with me so long that I feel a certain loyalty to it, evidently.

But whatever rod and reel selection the angler ends up with should be one that suits that angler. I heartily suggest that the beginner get out and practice *before* he gets on the stream and goes after steelheads, no matter with what type of rod and reel he intends to do his fishing. The streams are usually pretty well manned with other anglers and it is no place to do battle with mis-matched gear of any kind.

3 Steelhead Fly Equipment

My first love in fishing equipment is the fly rod. And like most other American fishermen, I consider the steelhead the epitome of angling trophies to be taken by the fly rod route. But, after many years of trying to show beginners how to use the specific techniques that have been developed strictly for steelhead fishing, I am getting discouraged.

The problems faced by the fly fisherman when he goes after steelheads are the same as those faced by the spin fisherman and the level-winder. He not only has to consider the potent problem of how to find his fish in the first place, but he will usually be faced with the job of making long casts in virtually 100 per cent of the setups he's likely to run across. When I tell a beginner at steelhead fly fishing that it's almost essential that he be able to make casts of 100 ft. or more with his fly rod, he looks at me like I'm out of my mind. Then, when I pick up the rods I normally use, make a cast of 100 ft. and try to show him how to do it, the thing really becomes complicated. But, with a few of the beginners, just seeing that line scream out there to these fantastic distances acts like a shot of adrenalin right into their veins, and I've got another steelhead fly fisherman on my hands. This is what keeps me in there plugging for new fly fishing talent.

In this chapter, as in the others, I will give specific outfits, complete with rod, reel, and line, and the exact reasonable distances that can be expected of them. These are figures that I can prove at any time, but the main reason that they are important is that the beginner will have something to gauge himself against—in short, if the outfit isn't giving him what I say it will, then he can be sure that there is something wrong with his own technique, and that it isn't a mismatched piece of gear that is causing the trouble.

But distance isn't the only element to this steelhead fly fishing game. I know of many anglers who do a reasonable job of catching their fish without much talent in the distance field. In fact, I'd say that the majority of fishermen who angle for the steelheads with a fly aren't more than modestly proficient as far as distance is concerned. My idea here is that distance fly casting and the ability to cast those extra 20 or 30 feet can never be a handicap, but usually it is the deciding element when it comes to any real measure of success.

Most fly fishermen who come to steelheading have had a lot of past experience on other species, such as black bass and trout. And it would seem that this should give them just that much of a head start in the whole game. Unfortunately, this isn't the case. I've found that surprisingly few of them can handle even the conventional fly outfits commonly associated with trouts, bass, or other kinds of fish with any measure of perfection. And, oddly enough, the few who are very proficient at casting are the hardest of the lot to teach the special techniques used by the better steelhead fly fishermen.

What I've run into with beginners at "long lining," as

I like to call the technique of casting a fly for long distances, is that they are not thinking of the whole thing in the right light. They have to be convinced that they are still casting a weight in fly fishing, the same as with any other kind of gear.

Here's how the the thing shapes up as it concerns the fly fisherman. For the sake of illustration, let's take two rods, one a spinning stick 9 ft. long and the other a fly rod 9 ft. in length. There is little difference between the two of them, and if we put on those weights, as I outlined in the last chapter, they will both bend about the same amount.

If the angler fits up the spin outfit with 8 lb. monofilament and ties on a 1/4 oz. lead weight he will be able to cast for short distances. If he then changes the weight of the sinker to a 1/2 oz., the distance he can reach is considerably increased. Then, suppose he works with weights from 3/4 oz., 1 oz. and on up to a point about 2 1/2 oz. where the rod will no longer have the built-in power to more than lift the weight off the ground, let alone cast it for any distance.

The point is that the weight used in casting with any rod is critical. With the average steelhead spin outfit there is only one weight, say 1 1/4 oz., that will give maximum distance with a minimum of effort. But with a fly outfit, the same rules apply, don't they? There is a certain point where the angler can bend his back into the cast—say a 3/4 oz. weight in this case—and still get the best distance he ever will be able to reach with that particular rod and line. If the weight is any heavier or any lighter, he will not be able to get everything out of that particular outfit.

The fly rod is no different than the spin or the level wind outfit. Any rod casts weight!

In fly casting it is a little harder to picture the weight element. *In casting a fly, the line is the weight!* The fly and the leader merely go along for the ride.

Now to get back to the fly rod and the spinning rod, both 9 ft. long. These rods are approximately the same when we test them with a static bend (as when we were choosing our spinning rods). It stands to reason that they should both have the same distance "built into them," doesn't it? But the fact that the fly weighs almost nothing complicates the matter. We've got to make up for this with a weight.

Again the weight in fly casting *is in the line*. So, if we have a 1/4 oz. line we can cast for a short distance—exactly the same as in the case of the identical spin rod. If we increase the weight to 1/2 oz. we should be able to cast a good deal farther. But sooner or later we run into the point where the line weighs too much for the rod. This is still exactly the same as the case of the spinning rod. The only real difference is that with a fly line the weight is spread out over a considerable length of heavy line, where a spinning weight is concentrated into a single blob of formed lead. And here is the point where the beginner becomes confused when we speak of casting weights as they concern fly lines.

First, the only fly line weight that we are interested in is that which is past the tip top of the rod. The weight of the line still left on the reel or still in the guides means nothing as far as the cast is concerned. Again, it is this weight in the line *past the tip of the rod* with which we false cast, which is important to the total distance we are trying for.

Second, the weight of the leader and the fly are not considered at all. They merely travel along wherever the fly line goes.

So, what modern steelheaders have done is to chop the end from a heavy fly line (using large enough line so that the total weight of the chopped off piece, usually 30 ft. long, is about equal to the same weight that would be used on the same size spinning rod) and tie it to a length of regular 20 lb. test monofilament line. This is what is known, in steelhead parlance, as a "shooting head" and a "shooting line." And these lines and heads are essential to modern day steelhead fly fishing.

Any fly fisherman knows that he can only support so much of a double taper fly line in the air with any given rod. He starts out false casting and on each successive cast he lets a bit of line shoot through the guides. Sooner or later he reaches the point where the weight of the line, plus the wind resistance, will cause the whole works to collapse around his ears. Now, this usually occurs long before he ever reaches anything like a 100 ft. distance.

The anglers who learned their fly casting trade on the east coast tried to get around this item by using weight forward lines. These weight forward—"torpedo taper"—lines can still do a fair job for most long distance fly casting, but western steelhead anglers use their shooting heads and shooting lines to reach out a great deal farther than the torpedo head fishermen ever will. Go to any distance casting event and you'll find that every distance fly caster is using a steelhead shooting head setup. In fact, most of the distance casting champions in the past 15 years are western anglers.

The fly fishing beginner at steelheading might wonder why there's all this concern with distance. Well, a single steelhead trip on a selection of western streams will give him the quickest answer. These streams are big and they have a lot of water in them. The shooting head and shooting line setup not only lets the angler cover a great deal more water, but it also has a built in water cutting ability (due to the fact that monofilament shooting line is less water resistant than any other material) that standard double taper or torpedo taper fly lines do not have. So, the setup also lets the angler fish deep in these powerful streams. At present there are two commercially available "Shooting Head" lines on the market. One is sold under the trade name of Stream King by the Sunset Company of Santa Rosa, California. The other is called a shooting taper and is made by Scientific Anglers of Midland, Michigan. But it is possible to make up a shooting head from any standard double taper line on the market.

The common process is to merely find a line make that is the right weight for the specific rod the angler is using. This was once a tough job, but now there is a standard system of marking fly lines that makes the job simple. About 1960, the fly line manufacturers, The Associated Fishing Tackle Manufacturers, got together to devise a new system of fly line designations set up on a basis of number rather than by letter, as it had been done before that time. Here is the table:

Standardized Fly Line Weights

Line Number	Weights in Grains	Minus and Plus Tolerance in Grains
1	60	54 – 66
2	80	74 – 86
3	100	94 – 106
4	120	114 – 126
5	140	134 – 146
6	160	152 – 168
7	185	177 – 193
8	210	202 – 218
9	240	230 – 250
10	280	270 – 290
11	330	318 – 342
12	380	368 – 392

Identification symbols: DT: double taper. L: level. WF: weight forward taper. ST: short single taper. F: floating line. S: sinking line. I: intermediate weight (for both dry-fly and wet-fly lines). All classifications are based on 30 feet of line measured under 1 lb. of tension.

The steelhead fisherman is primarily concerned with the fly line sizes from No. 6 at the minimum to No. 10 or No. 11. I have never personally seen anyone using a line heavier than a No. 11. Too, it will be a rare occasion when the serious steelhead man will have any use for a line that does not sink, though some fly fishermen still try their hands at fishing flies just under the surface.

I have personally owned and used about 50 fly rods with which I have taken steelheads. I have made just about every mistake in the book buying fly fishing equipment, and I am forever on the lookout for better fly fishing tools. But as it now stands, I have three rods that I use to the exclusion of all the others. And here is the rod, line weight, and manufacturer so that the beginner who doesn't have a personal prejudice or choice can judge for himself when he goes to buy his first steelhead fly stick. I definitely do not insist that these outfits are the best available, except for me personally. But, if the outfit the beginner does start out with does not cast a fly to approximately 100 ft. (on dry land), then either he isn't casting properly or the outfit he's using isn't properly matched. Any of the following three rods will cast a fly 100 ft. or more.

The first outfit is a FF109 Feralite rod made by Fenwick fitted with a 2A Sunset Stream King shooting head that weighs 288 grains. An alternate line is a Special A (GAG Double Taper) Wetcel that weighs 296 grains and is put out by Scientific Angler. I cut a 30 ft. section from either end of the double taper, splice a loop to the rear and make this line up into shooting heads.

The second outfit is built around a 9 ft. Lima Glas 1145 rod blank. The same lines handle well with this rod. All these outfits have 100 ft. of 20 lb. test monofilament and the spool filled with heavier line, normally nylon squidding line.

The other outfit is a bit lighter. A 9 ft. FF108 Feralite rod is fitted with an A Sunset Shooting Head or a GBG Wetcel, both at about 265 to 270 grains. The best Shooting Taper I've ever used for this outfit is an ST-10 Hi-D Scientific Anglers line, because it sinks so deep. I use this outfit when wind conditions let me get away with a lighter line.

The illustration shows how this setup is put together on the reel. One important item is that the steelhead man shouldn't use more than 100 ft. of 20 lb. test monofilament line. Then he should fill up the spool with fairly hefty squidding line, testing about 30 to 40 lbs. The reason for this is that steelheads are tough fish, and the water where they are taken is usually pretty strong. If the angler fills his spool with monofilament line, and the fish makes a long run, the angler will be forced to wind the line back under heavy pressure. (A steelhead is always fought from the reel, never by stripping line by hand.) With each turn of the reel the monofilament will pile on the spool of the reel under this stress, and it actually stretches and is smaller in diameter than it is when it isn't being stretched. After a couple of hundred turns of the spool the outward pressure on the side plates of the reel is so terrific that there is every chance in the world of them rupturing. I personally lost two reels this way before I figured out what was causing the trouble. And I have heard of anglers who have had the side plates blown completely off the reel.

And, as long as we're on the subject of reels, the only thing a steelhead fisherman needs is a good quality reel with plenty of capacity. Actually, the larger the reel the better, the way I see it. This isn't because the average steelhead will make extremely long runs, but rather because a large spool lets the line go on in larger and looser coils. The fly lines that are on the market today are very fine pieces of gear; they rarely have any coiling tendencies for more than a few minutes after they are in use. But monofilament will definitely take a set. And I've found that the larger coils that come with mono on a larger spool are just that much easier to straighten out.

The only other thing about reels that I think is important for the steelhead fly fisherman to consider is their weight. The lighter the reel for a given size, the better it is as far as I'm concerned. This works to the advantage of the money conscious angler because most of the heavier reels are more expensive than the lighter models. In fact, I splurged over $30 a while back for a beautiful new reel. But it is so heavy that I never use it. Most of the best reels will cost less than $15. One final thing about reels is to try to forget the old idea that a reel should "balance" a rod—this old-time idea that the reel should be heavy enough to "balance the rod at a point close to the handle" is ridiculous. There is no such thing. All an angler has to do is to go to any casting event and watch the boys who take everything into consideration, and see that the tournament casters never, ever, use a reel if the rules of event do not require them to. And the next time you have a tired arm from hours of casting, just take the reel off and stick it in your pocket. It feels like you just got a new start! So, the lighter the reel the better.

Now for the actual casting with a shooting head and shooting line setup: The process is simplicity itself, when you see it done. Basically, all you do is work the 30 ft. shooting head out of the guides, plus about three feet of the monofilament. You false cast once or twice and let it go. DO NOT WORK THE BACK END OF THE FLY LINE ANY FARTHER THAN SIX FEET PAST THE TIP TOP.

It's really quite a thrill to see the look on a man's face once he gets this rig into operation. If the man has some fly fishing experience he can automatically add at least 20 ft. to his distance once he gets the idea anchored in his mind. The main thing to remember is that you do not work the line out farther on successive casts; *you "shoot it" out all at one time!*

There are other elements to long lining that are important, but they are very difficult to explain and demonstrate to someone in person, let alone to try to explain in a text. But I've included some pictures of "double hauling" to get extra distance in another chapter, and I can only hope that the beginner can get the general idea from them. But the best possible way to learn this double haul system is to have it shown to you by someone who's been over the hurdles. Most organized casting clubs have members who can demonstrate the procedure. The next best thing I can say about this casting, or any other fly casting, for that matter, is if you are not getting good casts it's almost a certainty that the trouble is in your backcast. The only cure I've ever found is to turn around and look at that backcast.

Now that I've spent most of this chapter stressing the importance of distance casting for steelheads, I'll change the pace and say that the majority of fish will be caught within 50 ft. to 70 ft. of the angler. Any angler who can manage consistent casts of this distance—once he's actually on the stream—will not have too much trouble with steelhead fishing. But it's been my experience that very few anglers can reach this distance consistently when they are wading to their belly button, as they will most of the time.

Any angler who uses a torpedo taper line or a weight forward line can take his share of steelheads if he can use the gear effectively. In the hands of a good man, 90 ft. casts are fairly standard with these rigs, and the only real handicap in using them comes when the line is actually in the water. The thicker running line behind the torpedo taper will not cut down through the water nearly as well as the monofilament shooting line used on the modern steelhead rigs that I've outlined here.

Every year I see a few anglers doing pretty good work with the old standard double taper lines. However, these men usually have to hunt up a place where really long casts are not necessary in order to be able to cast over any fish at all. Too, they are virtually out of business during the winter months because these double taper rigs simply will not sink down enough to attract these fish which hug right next to the bottom. However, I do say that a fly fisherman shouldn't stay away from the stream merely because he doesn't have the modern equipment. It's far more logical to get out and fish with whatever the angler has than to sit back and wait until he can operate like a veteran.

4 Catching That First Steelhead

There is nothing in the fresh water fishing world that can quite compare with the sight and feel of a fresh run autumn steelhead on the other end of a rod and line. I am a great counter of jumps, and these fall run fish are the jumpingest, runningest things in fins. I rarely ever hook one of these babies that I don't end up with a final jump total of at least ten full leaps. And this doesn't count the wallowing and racing runs that are sandwiched in among the jumps.

Probably every angler who has ever fingered a fishing outfit wants to tangle with one of these fierce competitors. And, I think that it's easy to start out on any given year and still be successful in getting into the kind of fishing that most anglers are dreaming about. However, a steelheader has to be willing to play the game a certain way. If he wants to be successful within a reasonable length of time at steelheading, there are certain rules that he simply cannot ignore.

The first thing for the newcomer to think about when he actually sets out to take his first batch of steelheads is that these fish run up the coastal streams of the Pacific slope over a tremendous range. The commonly accepted range of serious steelhead streams is from just south of San Francisco on the California coast to the Aleutian Islands and the Alaska Peninsula. Within this range there is just about every conceivable size and type of water. The range of water types is actually pretty fantastic, from tiny brooks that purl through meadows to giant streams like the Columbia and Fraser which are more like moving bays than rivers.

Next, the prospective steelheader has to take the facts of weather change into consideration. In the vast majority of streams, rain or snow can completely change the entire character of each stream in a matter of hours. By the same token, rain can be good for some streams—because it freshens up the water in them and gets the steelheads into a moving and biting mood—and it can turn others into raging torrents which makes any serious attempt at fishing a farce.

It is also safe to say that somewhere within the range of the steelheads there is a run of fish going on at the very minute this book is being read. But there are prime times—those times that have been best in the past—when the steelheads are most likely to be in certain given streams. Now, without even going any further the prospective steelheader is already stuck with at least a pair of big variables—weather and type of water.

It would take more than one large book just to list the streams, their best dates for steelheads, and what usually happens to them at various stages of flood or drought. Not only that, but it wouldn't make much difference to the man who wants to go out and get into a run of fish. By the time the angler finished this book and walked to the corner tackle store, a storm could have moved into any of the areas and completely changed things from what they were an hour ago. But there is a practical way to go about this matter of getting into that first run —and any successive runs of fish. I use the system myself every year, and rarely ever get completely skunked if I've got a reasonable amount of time to fish, say two weeks (or an annual vacation for most of us).

Before a steelheader can ever hope to be *consistently* successful at the game of landing steelheads, he absolutely must give up the concept of "Great Steelhead Rivers." These are the rivers that have a history of being really productive. Just a few of the famous streams that ring through the mind of the serious steelhead man are the Eel and Klamath in California, or the Rogue and Umpqua in central Oregon; the Hoh and Queets are currently building a big reputation in Washington and the Kispiox in British Columbia is logging large catches of large fish. Any of these streams can produce good fish, but the angler who wants to take fish on the majority of trips must simply consider any of them as another stream into which steelheads run. If he doesn't, the odds are that he will have a long stint on the streams before he ever manages a hook up with a steelhead.

If the angler lives on the West Coast, or within easy striking distance of it, he has the first problem, that of being close to the stream, whipped. If the angler who wants to tangle with the steelheads lives a considerable distance away, in the Midwest or on the East Coast, he can still use my system, but he's got a bigger logistics problem to face. So, for the sake of having a workable example, let's say that we pick an angler from Minneapolis, Minn.

To keep things on a level keel, let's also say that our Minneapolis angler isn't a wealthy man. He has a reason-

able amount of money and a driving ambition to get into
the mighty steelhead. He also has a two week, annual
vacation from the factory where he works, and he can't
choose the exact time for taking this vacation. In other
words, he has to watch his budget and take the time
that's available to him. This is about as tough a way to
have to go about steelheading as you'll find. So for a
break, let's say that the Minneapolis angler at least has
a smidgeon of fishing knowledge—he's taken a few local
black bass and trout on occasion. This way we can skip
the basic requirements of knowing how to handle the
simplest fishing gear.

The first thing our Minneapolis angler should do is
to sit down and write a letter to the fish and game people
in the various states and provinces in Canada and the
U.S. where steelheads run at all. Here are the addresses:

Alaska: Bureau of Sport Fisheries, Box 2021, Juneau.

British Columbia: The Commissioner, Government Travel
Bureau, Dept. of Recreation and Conservation, Victoria; Also,
Office of the Game Commission, 567 Burrard St., Vancouver 1.

Washington: Dept. of Game, 600 N. Capitol Way, Olympia.

Oregon: Travel Information Division, State Highway Dept.,
Salem; Also, State Game Commission, 1634 S.W. Alder, Portland 8.

California: Conservation Education Section, Dept. of Fish and
Game, 722 Capitol Ave., Sacramento.

Idaho: Dept. of Fish and Game, 518 Front St., Boise.

I sent the following letter to these addresses:

Gentlemen:
I am interested in coming to your state (province in the case
of British Columbia) to take steelhead trout. I would like
very much to have some kind of advance advice on what you
consider the best time to come into your area. I would appreciate anything you can do to help me to arrive at the right

Top row, left to right: Admiral, Alaska Mary Ann, Alder, Bishop, Black Coachman, Black Demon.

Second row: Black Gnat Bucktail, Black Joe, Black Prince, Blue Bottle, Brown Mallard, Canada.

Third Row: Carson, Chambers, Cinnamon, Coachman Bucktail, Conch, Cumming's.

Fourth row: Deacon, Deer Fly, Dixie, Dodger, Dolly Varden, Dose.

Fifth row: Dugmore, Dusty Miller, Eel Optic, Emerald, Fall Favorite, Fern.

Top row, left to right: Fisher, Flight's Fancy, Fox, Gibson Girl, Gold Hilton, Golden Demon.

Second row: Golden Pheasant, Gordon, Gray Drake, Gray Jay, Green Drake, Hawk.

Third row: Hooker, Irish Turkey, Jock Scott, June Black, Kate, King Fisher.

Fourth row: Laramie, Light Edson Tiger, Major, Mallard, March Brown East, March Brown West.

Fifth row: March Dun, McGinty, McKenzie, Mickey Finn, Minnow, Gold, Montreal.

Top row, left to right: Moth, Oak, Orange Black, Pale Dun, Parmachene Belle, Piker.

Second row: Plath, Polar Shrimp, Poorman, Potter, Quaker, Railbird.

Third row: Red Ash, Rio Grande King, Sand Fly, Scarlet Ibis, Seth Green, Shrimp, Orange.

Fourth row: Silver Demon, Silver Doctor, Silver Ghost, Silver Hilton, Sock, Supervisor.

Fifth row: Teton, Thor, Thunder, Umpqua, Van Lueven, Victoria.

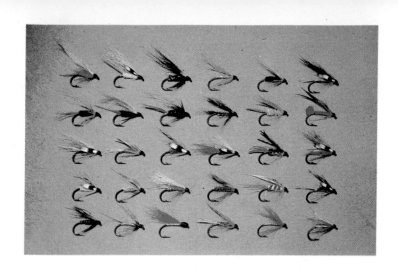

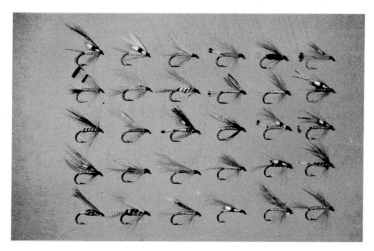

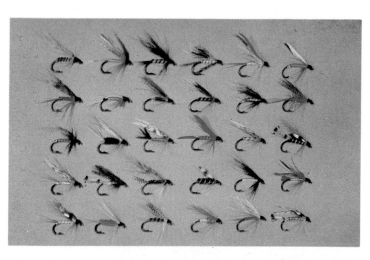

time. Also, anything you might suggest pertaining to the proper equipment normally used to take steelheads in your area would be greatly appreciated.
Thank you.

Here is the type of material these agencies will send from the various states and provinces:

From Idaho I got a personal letter:

Steelhead fishing starts to pick up here in September and gets pretty good about November. Although we have steelhead in our waters all winter, fishing success drops off generally until the latter part of March and April. Actually, fishermen are taking an occasional steelhead now in the Snake River near the mouth of the Clearwater River at Lewiston. However, in the last week or so warm weather and large floes of ice have complicated the fishing picture.

Most of the steelhead fishermen use a very heavy casting rod and a spinning reel. They seem to have the best success drift fishing in a boat. However, there are also many fishermen who have good success fishing from the bank. They use dare-devils, salmon eggs and similar types of lures.

Sincerely,
E. Kleiss Brown, Chief Information and Education
518 Front Street, Boise, Idaho

From California I got an informative map and folder that lists every single stream in the state which has a steelhead run, plus the gear normally used, and the best dates that these streams usually have fish in them. The map-pamphlet is called, "Salmon and Steelhead Fishing Map." Also, they included a copy of the fishing laws that are currently applicable, which is very necessary because the state has some waters closed to all fishing at certain times of the year.

From Oregon I received a personal letter:

I have enclosed two brochures where you will find considerable information on the salmon and steelhead possibilities in the state of Oregon. Of course, the greatest steelhead activity takes place during the winter months as these fine game fish come in from the ocean on their winter spawning migrations. The months of December through February are the best with the weather playing a key role in the angler success. Rains can come at any time during the winter along our coastal streams which can put them out of shape for fishing overnight. However, unless rains continue for a lengthy period most of the rivers usually clear up in a few days.

Summer steelhead angling is confined primarily to the Rogue, Umpqua and the Deschutes River systems. The brochure on fishing in Oregon will give you the approximate time of year that these runs appear.

A host of lures are used for taking steelhead including spinners, several varieties of wobbling or flashing lures along with flatfish, spin and glows, oaky drifters and others. Cluster eggs are a favorite on many of our streams. Long rods are preferred by most steelheaders using either spinning tackle or casting reels.

Sincerely,
Milt Guymon, Information & Education Division
P. O. Box 4136, 1634 S.W. Alder St., Portland 8, Oregon.

Also received was "Salmon Waters of Oregon" which also has a good deal to say about the steelhead fishing, though primarily concerned with the salmons. This pamphlet also has a good map showing many of the Oregon streams. Also, the pamphlet, "Fishing in Oregon" was included which pointed out steelhead waters and a few indications of the best dates, though it was liberally sprinkled with data on trout and salmons as well as bass and other fish.

From Washington State, I received a copy of the fish and game laws, plus three Washington State Game Bulletins which have some very pertinent dope on when the fish are in Washington streams, because Washington has a special punch card system of telling when and how many fish are being taken in that state. The dates of these bulletins are:

January, 1956, Vol. 8, No. 1, "His Excellency The Steelhead"

January, 1959, Vol. 11, No. 1, "Steelhead To Order" and "What Happened To Last Years Steelhead Season"

January, February, March, 1962, Vol. 14, No. 1, "Steelhead" and "Washington's Twenty-Five Top Steelhead Streams."

From British Columbia I received a Road Map of the province from both sources, Fishing, as well as Hunting Laws, "Guide to Sport Fishing Regulations in the Tidal Waters of British Columbia," a few miscellaneous brochures, a thick "British Columbia Tourist Accommodation Directory" which names virtually every motel or hotel in the province, plus such items as Ferry Routes, Boat Launching Sites, Trailer Camps, etc.

Then there were a sheaf of mimeographed sheets that did a good job of pinpointing the runs of steelheads for date and travel methods, plus several papers on the fishing in various local lakes. The Vancouver Island papers were particularly good. From Alaska, another personal note:

First, we have about 30 miles of road (this system is slowly extending) and are not able to drive to any real hot steelhead fishing. True, they run Ketchikan Creek which flows through town and Ward Creek just north of town but both are not what they once were. So, driving to Naha R., Thorne R., and Karta R., is a taxifare, an air taxi that is, which we use here very freely. Fares are not unreasonable.

Others probably as good are Fish Creek (21 miles), Lake McDonald Outlet (42 miles), and Klawak Creek (55 miles) to mention a few. All of the locations mentioned have shelters where an angler may comfortably spend several days. Naha, Fish Cr., Karta and Lake McDonald outlet may be reached and easily fished by boat having living quarters aboard.

Our steelhead are in the streams every month except possibly July. There is no closed season on them and the limit is the same as for trout with a possession allowance for 2 daily limits. There are very few fish taken here that run over 20 pounds. The best fishing is probably November but good by any standard most of the year. With the new ferry system, a non-resident angler is better fixed than ever before.

Sincerely,
Robert T. Baade, Sport Fish Biologist
1829 Tongass Avenue, Ketchikan, Alaska

Also received was a pamphlet, "National Wildlife Refuges in Region 6," that is virtually useless to the steelhead fisherman because it is concerned primarily with game and not fish.

It is a lot of informative material for only a small investment of time and effort. Some of it is of extreme importance and that in British Columbia in the "Directory" actually gives a fertile field for further correspondence, because just about any businessman would be glad to offer good advice to anyone who is coming into the area.

None of this material is very specific. Because nobody in their right mind would attempt to pinpoint runs of steelheads exactly. Rather, these are rough guides and perhaps suggestions that will act as a guide for anglers who are not familiar with the sport of hunting down a run of steelheads. Then again, all that the system has cost the angler from Minneapolis so far is a couple of postage stamps and a little effort. Still, he's managed to learn a good deal about where he can expect to find runs of steelheads.

In almost every case, the runs of steelheads will hit a series of rivers at approximately the same time. These prospects are pointed out in the material the angler already has in hand. The next step is to find out if there are two well separated areas that the angler can use for making two separate plans. For instance, the first fall runs of steelheads can be expected in the Klamath-

Eel-Smith-Trinity drainages in California's far northern counties about the middle or end of September. At this same time steelheads are expected in the Rogue-Umpqua drainages, in the mid-section of Oregon. The Queets-Hoh-Quinault loop in central Washington starts to get a play from the steelheads at about this time of year. And the Vancouver Island streams are starting to show promise. So, if the Minneapolis angler has his trip scheduled for late September he should start making final plans, using at least two of these general areas for a starter.

However, the Minneapolis angler should never choose two areas that are right next to each other geographically. In other words, he shouldn't start considering the northern California and central Oregon streams as his target and plan on reservations into these areas. If he does this, and if some kind of storm of considerable size should move in, there's every chance in the world of that same storm putting both of these areas out of commission at the same time. A better choice might be to really separate the two target areas and make Vancouver Island the first choice and the north California streams the second choice. Naturally, the end of September doesn't present such a bad weather threat during most years, but this trip is going to cost a fair piece of change to someone coming in from as far away as Minneapolis, so why take the chance without good reason?

The next logical step is to check with an airline or two which service the general areas the angler from Minneapolis is interested in. But it would be foolish to make definite reservations much more than a week before he plans to depart. A good piece of insurance that can be had cheaply is for the Minneapolis angler to buy newspapers from the largest daily newspaper in the main city that services the areas in which he's interested. A city the size of Minneapolis undoubtedly has this kind of out of town newspaper service available somewhere within the city. The reason he should go through the trouble to buy these papers from the big city dailies in his target areas is that the fish and game columnists on those papers will wax heavily if a run of fish is spotted in any of the nearby streams. Also they'll moan and groan if the fish do not appear when they are expected. In short, the Minneapolis angler can get as good information as an angler who lives within a few miles of the good steelhead water merely by investing a few dollars in out of town newspapers a few weeks before the expensive trip is to take place. This way the Minneapolis angler can make the final choice between the two areas.

The day or two before the angler is actually going to board the plane for the steelhead country, he'd be wise to spend another few dollars and make a phone call or two. He should place the phone call to the fish and game columnist in the local daily newspaper that he's been reading the last few weeks. It should be a person to person call, very definitely! A baseball writer or the sports staff editor might answer the phone. They might even say that the fishing is swell, but only the fish and game man knows for certain the latest dope on fishing conditions. It would be far better to phone back later and contact the specific man the angler is looking for than to get hold of the wrong man. I can guarantee that once the Minneapolis angler explains that he's about to make a long, expensive trip to the steelhead country, and would like to know what his chances of taking a fish are, that the fish and game man will tell the absolute truth. If he says that fishing is bad, believe him. It would be better to cancel the trip altogether than to go against this expert's word. And these men are expert at reporting on the fishing in their area. If they weren't they wouldn't last a month in this west coast area where every other human being totes a fishing rod.

So, if the Minneapolis angler has followed my system this far, he is finally ready to hop a plane for the land of the steelheads—that is, if the reports were encouraging. Flying, by the way, is the cheapest, quickest way for anyone to travel the distances we are speaking of here; and for an angler who only has two weeks to spend, the time element becomes very important. It's conceivable that it could still take the better part of that much time for a beginner to find and zero in on a run of fish, because he's going to have to learn a lot of actual on the stream lore in a fairly short time. But, air service gets a bit sticky and complicated when our Minneapolis man thinks about making charter flights into some of the tiny hamlets that sit on the shores of the best steelhead waters. I intentionally planned things this way.

I think that the man from Minneapolis shouldn't even consider staying in a resort or lodge right on the banks of any stream. If he did, he'd be stuck with fishing just that stream. Actually he'd be stuck with fishing a single section of that stream, and this would put all the odds against him because he's only got two weeks in which to find and catch his fish. Another thing, if a really worthwhile run of fish should enter any given stream, the local anglers who've got contacts with people right on the stream will appear like magic. They'll take up all of the available accommodations, and you can bet the resort and lodge operators will give them first consideration because they are old, established customers. It doesn't matter how many hundred accommodations there are available, they'll all be filled if a good run of fish moves in; westerners take their steelheading seriously!

Instead, our Minneapolis angler should plan to make his headquarters in any one of several large cities that are within easy striking distance of the better fishing streams. These large cities will have unlimited accommodations, and the next step in the plan, that of getting some kind of transportation once he has actually arrived, is a simple matter. The next step is to rent a car. These rentals are very reasonable and are a pretty small expense item if the Minneapolis angler has talked a couple of his buddies into making the trip with him so that they can split the bill two or three ways. Even alone he won't go broke.

Here are the cities I think are logical spots in which to set up headquarters; and they all are near a good number of choice steelhead water. Also, car rentals are a simple matter in any of them:

Anchorage, Alaska: Willow R., Russian R., Newhalen R., Brooks R., Kvichak R., Wood R., Naknek R., Bristol Bay Tributaries.

Ketchikan, Alaska: Karta R., Thorne R., Naha R.

Vancouver, B.C.: Chilliwack R., Coquihalla R., Vedder R., Chehalis R., Campbell R., Oyster R., Cowichan R., Little Qualicum R., Pear R., Squamish R., Seymour R., Capilano R., Indian R., Ash R., Thompson R., Coquitlam R.

Seattle-Tacoma, Washington: Sol Duc R., Elwah R., Dungeness R., Skokomish R., Dosewallips R., Duckabush R., Deschutes R., Nisqually R., Puyallup R., Green R., Stillaguamish R., Skykomish R., Skagit R., Nookstack R.

Aberdeen, Washington: Willapa R., Chehalis R., Humptulips R., Quinault R., Queets R., Clearwater R., Hoh R., Fogachiel R., Calawah R., Satsop R.

Astoria, Oregon: Trask R., Wilson R., Kilchis R., Miami R., Tillamook R., Nehalem R., Necanicum R., Columbia R.

Portland, Oregon: Klickitat R., White Salmon R., Wind R.,

Washougal R., Lewis R., Kalama R., Cowlitz R., Elokomin R., Nemah R., John Day R., Willamette R., Deschutes R.

Newport, Oregon: Alsea R., Yaquina R., Siletz R., Nestucca R., Santiam R.

Coquille, Oregon: Smith R., Chetco R., Pistol R., Rogue R., Illinois R., Elk R., Sixes R., Coquille R., Umpqua R., Siuslaw R., Melolius R.

Redding, California: Upper Klamath R., Scott R., Salmon R., Trinity R., Yuba R., Feather R., Butte Cr., Deer Cr., Mill Cr., Antelope Cr., Battle Cr., Sacramento R.

Eureka, California: Lower Trinity R., Middle Klamath R., Lower Klamath R., Salmon R., Chetko R., Smith R., Redwood Cr., Mad R., Van Duzen R., Eel R., Bear R., Mattole R.

San Francisco, California: American R., Consumnes R., Mokelumne R., Toulumne R., Stanislaus R., San Joaquin R., Sacramento R., Papermill Cr., Salmon Cr., Russian R., Gualala R., Garcia R., Brush Cr., Alder Cr., Elk Cr., Greenwood Cr., Navarro R., Albion R., Big R., Noyo R., Ten Mile R., Santa Clara R., San Gregoria R.

Any of these large cities also have facilities for renting house trailers of modest size along with the rented automobiles. It would be a good move for a man like our Minneapolis angler to add this expense to his budget. First of all, the small house trailer will make him virtually independent of any kind of local accommodations and once he finds a run of fish he can settle down and really do some serious, on the spot, fishing. Too, the house trailers all have eating and storage features that will simplify these needed items.

But, before our Minneapolis man goes and rents a car and trailer, it would be a good move to make simple phone calls to the newspaper man he talked to long distance from home and to any other contacts he's managed to make in the large city he has chosen. This way he can get the latest dope on how and where the fishing is. Too, I wouldn't be surprised if he didn't get some kind of additional information that might save him a good deal of searching around. It's this matter of searching out runs of steelheads that will take up most of his time for the next two weeks or so.

Most good steelhead streams on the Pacific Coast have roads running right along their banks. The simplest thing for an out of town angler to do is to get a road map and start driving along these roads. What he is looking for is some kind of action among the local fishing population. It's a pretty good bet that these local boys will know where and when the fish have entered the stream. In fact, if the man from Minneapolis doesn't see a river getting a pretty good play from the local boys, it's a good indication that the fish aren't in that river, or at least aren't in that particular stretch of river. And he doesn't have enough time to simply wait a run out. He has to keep moving both upstream and downstream and from river to river until he does actually see, with his own two eyes, some kind of fishing action.

It may gripe a man trained on trout or black bass to consider the fact that he must follow the crowds to get into the fish, but this is one of the essential points about steelhead fishing that it is absolutely necessary for the beginner to learn and to stick to. Steelhead fishing can be just as good a few feet from a super highway as it is miles back in the woods. That's the way steelhead fishing is and probably the way it always will be.

Now, one last thing for the newcomer. If he doesn't own the equipment I outlined in the preceding chapters, he shouldn't buy it before he makes the trip to the steelhead country. It is much more logical for him to wait until he gets on the scene of action and to buy the things he will need right on the spot from the tackle dealers that are set up in all the local towns. He won't spend any more money by doing this, and he will be sure of getting the right tools for the job he's got to do.

Steelhead fishing, at least until an angler has had several years of experience at the game and knows a few out of the way spots, is a gregarious business. However, the beginner should welcome crowds rather than ignore or resent them. It's just like having a bunch of bird dogs to point the game out for him; and it can keep the beginner from stumbling around blindly and ending up fishing water that doesn't have a supply of fish in it at the time he happens to be there. This is the thing that keeps so many prospective steelheaders from taking fish the first few years after they get interested in it.

Everything that we've said here about the out of state steelhead fisherman also applies to the beginning angler who lives in the steelhead country—with the exception that the native angler doesn't have the added expense of travel that a man from as far as Minneapolis would be faced with. Our whole project in this chapter has been to take the toughest possible situation and show that it is still possible for a beginner to take fish within a reasonable amount of time.

In following chapters we'll talk about some of the techniques commonly used for actually fishing the streams of the Pacific Coast.

5 Steelhead Fishing Methods

The angler who decides to try his hand at steelhead fishing will eventually find that he doesn't really have much to say about which of the several methods of fishing he will end up practicing on any given stream. The type of water and the condition of the water at the time he is on the stream will dictate the method of fishing in the vast majority of cases. A fly fisherman, for instance, will find that he is also faced with the matter of getting some kind of backcast in certain kinds of fishing. For this reason—a large percentage of the streams and even pools on most streams will have high brush or rocks along the near shoreline—the fly fisherman is starting out with an added handicap before he ever wets a line.

Steelheads have the habit of being partial to specific locations and sections of any stream. There can be several miles of water that may look ideal to the angler, and yet the water will be barren of fish. Only the steelheads know exactly why they refuse to stop or hold in these sections. In fact, many spots will hold fish at one stage of water level and not at another. But most of these spots have long ago been found by local anglers, and the problem becomes one of watching and contacting these local fishermen in any new stream, rather than pioneering new or unusual methods of fishing new spots.

To the beginner, all the water looks alike, but it would be wrong to simply adopt one single method of fishing and try to use it in any holding pool or riffle he might happen to be fishing. One possibility is for the beginner to merely watch how the local fishermen are working the water and to try his best to duplicate it as closely as possible. This might sound easy, but in most cases it is a matter of watching for those little things that make certain local anglers great fishermen, as against the average local angler who only stumbles on fish occasionally. I've found that the myth of the ability of local anglers is exactly that, a myth! Most of these local people are very run of the mill anglers, or they are downright poor fishermen. But the few local boys who are good are easy to spot—they catch fish almost 100 per cent of the time!!

There are only a few general methods of fishing used for steelheads throughout their entire range. And probably the simplest, and the least effective, method of fishing for steelies is called by the adequate name of "plunking."

The very name, plunking, is descriptive of this method of steelheading. The angler merely hangs a heavy weight on the line, attaches bait, and slings the whole works out into a convenient body of water—normally a big, slow pool of water that is locally known for holding fish. When the heavy sinker, necessary to anchor the bait to the bottom, hits the water, it does so with a plunk. The rest of the method is simplicity itself. The plunking angler usually cuts a forked stick, builds a fire, and either stares at nothing or chats with other steelhead fishermen who are also plunking. Of all the methods of steelheading yet developed, plunking, in this way, is probably the least efficient. The only reason it is logical at all is that some areas have adopted the method, apparently for social reasons. But I have seen a few creative plunkers work the water, and while the method is still not very productive, there are a couple of ways to at least give it some added charm.

The biggest drawback to conventional plunking tactics is that it lacks mobility. Another drawback is that there is usually a fairly long waiting period between the cast and plunk of the heavy sinker and the time when the frightened fish will calm down enough to start considering a shot at the bait. I have personally sat on high banks opposite a group of plunkers and had a chance to see the effect on the fish when the water was clear and calm. When the necessary heavy sinker crashes into the water the fish instantly start darting around, usually either retreating to the deepest part of the pool or at least swimming as far away from the disturbance as possible while still remaining in the pool. It usually takes at least ten minutes for the disturbed fish to calm down and resume their natural hold in a pool. Long before the ten minutes are up, another plunker casts, or the first plunker will reel in, rebait or inspect his bait, and start the whole scaring procedure over again. Actually, the fish will even completely leave a pool if this kind of harassment keeps up long enough, and if there is a route of escape open to them. It's amazing that any fish at all are ever taken when plunking under these conditions.

The best cure for this heavy weight problem is to merely change to lighter tackle. This makes sense because the water, in any given stream that is suitable for plunking at all, is almost always pretty slow moving. Without a heavy current an angler stands a much better chance of landing any steelhead he manages to hook on light tackle, than he would if he were working fast moving water. So, in most plunking pools an angler using 6 lb. or even 4 lb. test line can be reasonably certain of landing even the largest steelheads—that is, if he has any real ability with his equipment and does not panic. Line that tests from 4 lb. to 6 lb. can do good work with weights that add up to no more than around ¼ oz. in most cases. And the steelies in the majority of pools aren't much bothered by a ¼ oz. terminal setup landing in the water.

But to get back to the big drawback in plunking, the lack of mobility. It is difficult to make any real dent in this drawback because as soon as the angler starts to move the bait around, he stops being a plunker and becomes a "drifter"—the main method of taking steelheads throughout the entire range. However, I have seen some pretty tricky things done by talented plunkers when they started using sliding sinker rigs.

A sliding sinker is a pretty delicate setup for most beginners to master. The basic idea is that the angler use weights designed for the job. But it is a simple procedure to merely tie a common split ring on the line after it has been passed through the hole in the middle of a sliding sinker or through the eye of a conventional sinker. Then he ties a short length of leader to the end of the line and a hook to the far end.

When the line is reeled in for a cast, the weight rests against the ring eye. When it is cast and settles to the bottom, the line runs freely through the eye or hole, and the bait is moved along the bottom by the current. This item of movement is very critical, and often it is necessary for the angler to attach a small cork or plastic float to the line just ahead of the bait in order to get the bait to move at all. But, if the float is too large, the bait will rise from the bottom and out of the feeding zone of the steelheads which is right next to the bottom. If it is too small, the weight of the hook and bait will anchor it to the bottom, and the whole affair is useless. Also, the angler has to accurately judge the strength of a current down next to the bottom which he cannot see. In all, sliding sinker fishing takes a great deal of experience and a lot of concentration—right down to making sure that the bait is always the same size, etc. But, in certain areas, as where the fish are laying back under a deeply cut bank, this sliding sinker rig is the only efficient method of snaking a bait to the fish. And, when it works, the results can be spectacular.

As a last resort, the plunker can always provide mobility to his bait—or in this case, even to a lure—by merely reeling the terminal tackle slowly in to the rod tip. In this cast-reel plunking, the talented anglers try to use as little weight as possible. The determining element is that the bait or lure must be kept on the bottom. This necessity of keeping the bait down on the bottom can be very trying on the nerves of an angler because these rigs will certainly find every snag in a pool. But, as we'll see in the following, the steelhead man who is losing rigs is usually the one who is also taking fish consistently.

The primary method of taking steelheads, wherever they are fished for, is by drift fishing. Drift fishing is nothing more than casting, letting the lure settle to the bottom, normally in moving water as in a riffle or the head of a pool, and letting a bait or lure tap along bottom with the current. This is an oversimplified rundown on drifting, because it is actually a very delicate art.

Now that spinning tackle has taken such a hold on the American angler, drift fishing has gotten a big boost in popularity. Before World War II, the drift fisherman had to use level wind reels. In those days the vast majority of level wind reels couldn't compare with the delicate, precision products we see on the market today. The spools on these old reels were mostly made of heavy metal. This forced the steelhead drift fisherman to use comparatively heavy weights in order to get those heavy reel spools revolving on the cast. The heavy weights then sank quickly to the bottom, where it took all the skill an angler could manage just to keep it bouncing along the bottom. And because of these things, the steelhead drift fisherman of those days was more or less forced to fish only the swiftest water in the riffles and the very heads of the pools. But now the level wind and the spin fisherman can go about as light as he wants, and he can fish just about any kind of water he happens to come across.

In drift fishing the angler can fish with either bait or lures, his basic terminal tackle is the same. A three-way swivel is attached to the line. A leader, usually about 18 in. in length, is attached to another ring on the three-way swivel. The last ring on the swivel is attached to a weight, just enough to take the whole works to the bottom and yet let it keep bouncing and rolling along the bottom by a length of line from 6 to 8 in. in length. (Some anglers use a ring-eye in the place of the three-way swivel, but the idea behind the rig is the same.)

Most beginners at steelhead drift fishing make the same basic mistake when they start out for a session of fishing.

They tie up their terminal tackle with a convenient size weight and go on fishing all the water available with this same weight. And yet, anyone who stops to think about the process of tapping a weight lightly along the length of any stream will quickly realize that it would be impossible to do this with any single weight. But, it is difficult to even explain exactly what a beginner is looking for when he starts "nodding" a rod for steelheads.

The term nodding refers to the action of the tip of the rod as the weight—which is towing the bait or lure to the bottom in the first place—bumps along the stones or gravel of the bottom. This ability to feel and sense the correct tempo of these transmitted bumps in the rod itself is the actual measure of the steelheader's ability. Personally, I like to work a rod at a tempo of one nod for each second of drift. If anything, the beat should be faster, rarely slower in good drift fishing water.

I usually watch the tip of the rod with my eyes as well as feel the weight bouncing along the bottom. I hold the rod tip up at about a 30 to 45 degree angle for two reasons: (1) I've found that this is the best angle to let the tapping of the bait be transmitted directly to the rod tip; (2) with the rod tip this high, I can instantly drop it from 2 ft. to 5 ft. when I feel the tapping rhythm broken. This matter of rhythm stopping is critical in steelhead drift fishing, especially with bait, but to a certain extent, even with lures.

As the angler works the bait or lure along the bottom the weight sort of hops and glides from the top of one rock to the next. In this way it gives a fairly accurate plot of the bottom to an angler who is sensitive to the rhythm of the tapping weight as it is transmitted to the rod tip. If the tapping suddenly stops for a few beats there is only one conclusion the angler can draw; the bait of lure is passing over a hole. And every steelhead in that stretch of the river will be in these holes, below the force of the current. So, by merely lowering the rod tip, it is possible for the angler to drop the bait or lure down into the indicated hole and let the fish have a chance to strike at it before the current, working on the line, pulls it out again. In many cases, I've found it necessary to hold a few feet of extra line in my off-rod hand so that I could not only drop the rod tip—and get about 5 ft. of extra drift—but by adding the extra line from the off hand, I can virtually drop the bait or lure straight down into a deep hole.

Now to get back to the weights used in drift fishing and their effect on the way different parts of a stream are fished. An angler who takes his drift fishing seriously usually has a large selection of weights with him when he is fishing. Too, he usually goes through the extra trouble of adding a fairly large snap swivel eye to the end of the dropper strand on the terminal tackle. This way, he can (and more important, will) change to different weights to suit the water speed and to try at all times to keep rhythm of the tapping approximately the same, or about one to the second.

Most drift fishermen that I've watched and fished with normally only fish the riffles and the very heads of the pools, where the current is still fairly strong. This would indicate that the average angler cannot get a decent drift in slower water and that they are obviously using too much lead to take the lure or bait to the bottom.

Another thing I have noticed about the way the average steelhead fisherman works the water is that he seems to think that all of the fish are on the other side of the river. Nothing could be farther from the truth. The proper way to go about working a stretch of water is to clip on a weight that the angler believes is a bit light. Then he should make a short cast and see if it is enough to take the lure, plus the weight, to the bottom. If it does, and if the rhythm of the tapping is approximately correct—one tap to the second—then the angler should stick with this weight for about three or four consecutive casts, or until he is casting it as far as it can be thrown. If he can quarter the stream clear to the further bank with this light weight, he shouldn't change it. If he finds that there is a point where he cannot reach the far side of the stream or where the rhythm (due to the force of the current acting on the extended line) is broken or slowed, he should change to a slightly heavier weight and keep increasing the weight until he has gotten the tapping rhythm back again. But this is only the first step in talented drift fishing.

The correct way to work a stretch of water is to go through the weight changing routine first at the head of a riffle; if no strikes come from this, the angler should take a few steps downstream (usually two or three steps will be enough) and go through the procedure again. This series of casts-three-steps downstream routine continues as the drift fisherman works his way down the length of the riffle. And, if the angler will take the time to keep his various weights conveniently at hand and makes sure to tie a good-sized snap to the end of his dropper strand, he won't find the process too time consuming. Too, he'll have given any fish in that stretch of the stream a good look at his bait or lure; whereas, the angler who uses only a single weight can't have given more than a small percentage of the fish an equal chance.

Another thing about the drift fishing terminal rig that is important is that the dropper strand that actually connects the sinker to the three-way swivel should be of material that tests a good deal less than the main line and the leader. For instance, a good combination of line weights would be 10 lb. monofilament for the main line and the leader, but the dropper strand should be of material that doesn't test more than 6 lb. This way, if the sinker hangs up on a snag (which it will more often than will the lure or bait) a sharp pull on the main line testing almost twice as much will break that weaker line on the sinker, and the angler will get his expensive lure or the bait back. The result is loosing a weight worth a few pennies instead of a lure worth 50 cents or more.

Now, the drift fisherman, who has a large supply of weight sizes along with him when he is fishing, can also fish well down into even the largest, stillest pools. And it is common knowledge among steelheaders who have many years at the game, that some of the largest fish nearly always hold at the place where the current from the riffle starts to curl off into the slower portion of the pool. This is such a productive area of any stream that it would even pay an angler to carry an extra spool of very light line, plus the necessary collection of light sinkers, so he can work this area of the streams properly. On modern spin reels it is a short job to change to a lighter spool of line, and it's definitely worth the effort, once the angler sees some of the huge fish that are caught this way.

One more point that concerns modern day steelhead fishing. Before World War II there was far less competition on the west's steelhead streams. In those days most of the anglers who did any steelheading at all normally had a good deal of fishing experience; and because the water that is good for steelhead fishing is comparatively limited, all the anglers were used to "rotating" through a riffle or run of water. The first angler would start at the head of a riffle or run, make a few casts, and take a few steps downstream, continuing the procedure until he had worked his way completely through all the water available—just as I indicated that the beginning drifter should work the water in a riffle if he has the chance to do it this way. But, the modern steelhead runs are hit by ten to fifty times the fishing pressure that the same runs had to bear up under in those other days. Plus, the angler talent is much different than it was back before the war.

Now it is not at all uncommon for fishermen to stop in any area of a riffle and refuse to move (something that in the old days would have gotten a rock bounced off his head) and the rest of the fishermen are forced to either work around that angler or to take up a stand somewhere else in the riffle. This is not a good way to take fish in a steelhead stream, because each riffle only has a few feet of its length that holds fish consistently. So, if the beginner runs into this kind of a setup—as he undoubtedly will—the only thing he can do is to watch the exact spot where a few of the anglers are catching fish; then he can either wait until that kind of fisherman leaves for the day or he can make sure that he is first man on the riffle the next morning. This is a discouraging thing, but that's the way the modern steelhead fishing is shaping up, so it's better to admit it than it is to fight the thing.

This item, of watching where in a run the fish are hitting, can be a very important element in steelheading success, even if the angler is fishing in water that doesn't have any other fishermen on it at the time. I've found that most of the good stealhead holds are either behind some kind of underwater obstruction, or they are normally located about three-quarters of the way down the full length of the average run. So, the steelheader should look for the telltale curl of a sunken rock or log and for the slick about halfway down the riffle that tells him that some kind of depression in the bottom is causing the water to flatten out at that spot. This way, he can avoid the time consuming job of fishing the top half of the riffle, which only in rare cases holds fish in a feeding mood. However, until the beginner has managed to take at least a few fish, the best procedure is usually to fish all the water from the top to the bottom of the riffles.

Fishing a fly in a steelhead stream has been glorified in many texts and in magazine articles without number. But, the problem of the drift fisherman—that of moving the lure as slowly and as deeply as possible—is exactly the same as that faced by the fly fisherman. The big difference between the two methods of fishing a steelhead stream is that the fly fisherman has the built in handicaps of not being able to work his fly as deep in as many places as the spin or level wind fisherman; he is limited to fur and feathers to tempt his fish (and thus limited to fishing water with at least a margin of visibility), and he always has to face the job of getting a place on the stream where he can make a backcast.

We'll go into the problem of getting the fly deep in a current in a later chapter, but here we'll say that the fly fisherman usually has to be a far better wader than the lure or bait fisherman. Later we'll discuss how to get a fly to dredge deep through the water (or for that matter, how to keep it near the surface when the angler finds the right conditions) by using weighted lines, fuse lead wire on the flies, and flies built on heavy wire hooks. Too, there are a few ways that the man with the fly rod can use bait and lures to get around those times when feather simply will not produce strikes from the steelies. Getting a backcast is actually the measure of a steelhead fly fisherman's total talent. Some of the best pools and riffles I've ever fished in are usually overlooked by other fishermen simply because I've worked out a way to make a modified "steeple cast" and still get long casts.

The fly fisherman should work the water in a run, riffle, or pool exactly the same as a bait fisherman would, as far as water coverage is concerned. He starts his casts short, at the head of a run or riffle. He lengthens line as far as necessary, or as far as he can reach if he is working a very large stream. Then he takes a few steps downstream and repeats the process until he reaches the break into the pool. The head of the pool is as important to him as it is to a bait or lure fisherman, and actually, he has a better chance of catching the lunkers that lay at the upper edge of the moving water than does the lure or bait man. And, if he runs into the same situation of the other fishermen being in the meat holes and refusing to rotate, he is also stuck with waiting until these men leave or making sure he's first on the riffle tomorrow morning.

There are many special techniques for taking steelheads that are a modified version of the drift and plunk fishing I've outlined in this chapter. There are ways of "nymphing" steelheads that pay off big in small, clear, and brushy streams. There are ways of "dropping" extra line when the angler senses a deep hold or where the fish are lying under cut banks that will add fish to the fly fisherman's bag, the same as it will to the lure or bait fisherman's stringer.

An angler can "crawl a bait" into the mouths of those big winter steelies that lay in big flat pools that hardly any other fishermen try. But there is a logical way to go about all steelheading that should prove informative to even the oldest hand at the game.

6 Systematic Steelhead Fishing

Steelhead fishing can be a hit and miss proposition if the angler doesn't adopt some kind of systematic way to go about his job of searching out the available water for the fish. This is particularly true if the angler is new to a given stream. For instance, it is entirely possible for the average beginning fly fisherman to fish a single stream for a period of several weeks without ever feeling the surge of a good steelhead on the other end of the line. But, I've developed what I believe is a logical, systematic way to go about the job of locating fish in any kind of stream, large or small.

My own personal aim is always to find water where I can take the steelheads with a fly. But I long ago admitted that the fly outfit is simply not the tool to use when I'm searching out a new stream with which I am not familiar. In most cases, I spend the first few days on any stream with a spinning rod. If it is small or average sized stream, I will normally choose a standard 7 ft. spinning rod fitted with a standard fresh water reel and 10 to 12 lb. monofilament line. If the water is large, such as the Klamath in California or the Rogue in Oregon, I will set up a 9 ft. rod with the same standard fresh water reel.

I habitually will use lures in preference to bait for this job of working a new stream. This is not a matter of snobbishness about the use of bait, but 20 years of fishing for steelheads has shown me that lures will cover many times the water that can ever be covered by serious bait fishing. Bait, in my opinion, has a very specific place in steelhead fishing, but covering water is not that place.

The first day on the new river, I will have several types of lures with me. I like to have at least a dozen lures of the flatfish type: this type of lure includes Guppy and Cinch Bugs, etc. These lures I consider the best type for use in water that is reasonably clear, but they work well in water that is quite a bit discolored. I also take a dozen or more of the Cherry Bobber type of lures. These lures are floating imitations of salmon egg or steelhead roe clusters normally, but they also include such models as the Spin-N-Glo, Okie Drifter, as well as the old favorite Cherry Bobber. Both of these groups of lures are natural floaters, and there are at least a hundred variations on the theme. I have settled on these particular models because they are easy to obtain almost anywhere steelheads are found, and they are about as productive as any of the other type.

Also in my creel I will have at least a dozen Wobble-Rite and Daredevel type lures and another dozen weighted spinner lures such as the Mepps or Hepp models. These lures are old favorites on many streams— usually the streams with a fairly heavy head of water—

but the important thing about them from my own personal standpoint is that they are compact, heavy enough to cast easily, and they do a good job of cutting down through the water to search out hidden fish.

My last selection of lures, for systematically working a new river, is merely a collection of Yarn Flies. These go by different names in different areas, but simply enough they are merely red wool yarn tied on single, double, or treble hooks. Personally I like the ones tied on double hooks and rarely ever use those tied on trebles because I can see no advantage to them, and I have found that they tear out of a fish easier than either of the others— probably because none of the hooks ever get a chance to take a good bite of flesh. At any rate, I use these cheaply tied yarn flies almost exclusively now because I have found that the fish will hit them as readily as they will bait, and they have the added diabolical charm of hanging up in the teeth of any fish that samples them.

This may seem like a huge selection of equipment to cart along on a day's fishing, but it is actually only a part of what I personally take with me in a small war surplus gas mask container around my waist. I have many maverick lure types that I am forever testing and trying out in different situations, and I find that the gas mask container is big enough to cart them along without wearing me out in the slightest. The important thing is to have a variety of lures and lure types to offer the fish in any new stream. Once I get to know a river or creek I may only carry one type of lure or will change over to fly fishing exclusively, but when I start out I want as good a chance as possible of getting into at least some fish within a reasonable length of time.

I carry roughly a hundred miscellaneous weights of two or three different types. I have a couple of dozen extra three-way swivels and snap swivels, plus knives, clippers, hook pliers, and an amazing collection of junk that I haven't touched in years. But my method of going about the day's work of actually fishing a new stream rarely varies.

First, I try to get on the stream as early in the morning as possible. I do this in spite of the fact that I've found that I catch just as many steelheads, in most streams, in the middle of the day as I ever have either early in the morning or late in the afternoon. The big reason I get out early is that I want to have as much *time* available as possible to go about this serious business of searching for the fish.

The next project is to choose a lure type to start out the day. I rarely hesitate here, unless some feature of the water interferes with my own preference; I normally choose the spinners or wobblers—merely because they are the simplest to use and require the least trouble to get into operation and to keep in operation. They also will cover more water than either of the other types. However, if the river or creek is very small or the water very mild, I have found that these wobblers and weighted spinners are too hard to keep working without hanging up on the bottom; they sink too fast.

If the water is very discolored I will invariably choose the Spin-N-Glo type of lure that whirls very rapidly in even mild flows and seems to attract fish no matter how dirty the water. If the water is mildly discolored, I would choose a flatfish type of lure for the early part of the day. Anyway, once I get started I literally "fish by the mile."

However, before I go further with my fish-by-the-mile system of working over the water in a new stream, let me qualify it a bit. The basic idea of this fish-by-the-mile technique is that I want to cover many pools, riffles, and stretches of the river in a short length of time. But the system is by no means cut and dried in its application. If I have been lucky enough to get some kind of local information from a salesman in a tackle store, the desk clerk at a hotel, the garage man, or any other person who might just conceivably have some kind of useful information as to where the fish "might" be found, I will do everything possible to put myself in these spots before I ever start fishing the water blindly. Too, though I don't trust too much the vast majority of local fishing information as far as it concerns the methods that are best, if some likely sounding local technique seems to me to make sense, I will start out trying it rather than trying to choose my own method on pure speculation.

Actually, it is very rare that a serious steelhead fisherman has to start out on a new river without some kind of local information. If nothing else, he can always look up the local tackle dealer and ask his advice, and a few judicious words at the local tavern or restaurant the evening before will often bring out worthwhile local information. The one piece of local advice that I've learned to ignore, especially as far as terminal tackle is concerned, is when I am told that bait of one kind or another is the *only* thing that will produce. And if the advice also includes the use of common plunking tackle and techniques, I will absolutely ignore it. I've found that a vast percentage of local fishermen fall into the plunking-bait fishing category and that the number of men who actually know their business in this line are so scarce as to make finding them almost impossible. Too, almost 100 per cent of the men who actually are competent, finished bait fishermen are almost invariably the type of angler who guards his hard earned knowledge as if it were a new chemical process of great value. This does not mean that these people cannot tell the angler, new to the stream, where he will "probably" find the fish.

Once I am on the stream I subconsciously divide the water into separate divisions: the riffles that are deep and fairly strong in the central currents attract me at once. These strong, deep (from 3 ft. to 12 ft.) riffles, experience has shown me, usually hold the majority of good fish that are in a feeding mood; they are also the best spots to work with spin fishing tackle. This does not mean that most of the fish in the river are in these spots— actually many more fish are usually holding in the shoals at the heads of the biggest, deepest pools during most of the year. But the deep riffles are easy to spot and I prefer to work them over most others. I would say that I devote most of my serious effort to them, due strictly to my own personal experience.

The next prime holding area is the heads of pools where the water from the riffle above is starting to curl out. If I also see a couple of good fish surfacing, rolling, or jumping in this area, I fish it with extra caution.

In a deep pool I usually fish along very quickly, merely casting out and reeling in as I move along. I have no doubt that there are probably several good fish in this still, deep water, but it's only rarely that I've ever caught them with lures and spinning tackle within a reasonable length of time.

The glide of fast water, just at the head of a new riffle, sometimes is a prime area to fish especially if there is a good run of fish moving through it or there are a few sunken obstructions there. But I would want some kind of special information before I would spend very much time during those first few days on a stream fish-ing these slicks. I usually move right along in these places and merely make a couple of hopeful casts into them as I move quickly past.

On every stream there are fishy-looking spots that just beg to have a lure cast into them. If I get a hunch about a swirl, slick in a riffle, or deep water shelving off into a rapid, I stop long enough to try my hand at sneaking a lure into them. But I have to force myself to move along to a new area after only a few reasonable attempts to work these places. It is essential that the angler merely put these places in the back of his mind for future reference and not waste too much time on them in the beginning.

This may all sound like an uncivilized way to go about the gentle art of angling to a man who has had most of his experience on delicate trout waters, but I've wasted at least half of my steelhead angling time trying to fish steelhead streams as though they were trout waters and have finally found that the two aren't very much alike. The thing for the beginner to remember is that he is dealing with an unknown body of water where the fish only hold in a relatively few specific spots and his job, if he's going to be successful within a reasonable length of time, is to find these few spots in the shortest possible time.

At the same time that I work quickly along a length of stream I am constantly on the lookout for those places where some other kind of tackle should be used. Naturally, my own first concern is in finding water that looks good for fly fishing gear; but I also keep an eye open for those places where the distances are great enough or the current strong enough to demand the use of a big level wind outfit. I've found that most streams fall into certain molds. Some of them have a good deal of

open, fly fishing water. Others are big monsters that beg
to be worked by a big meat rod—in these cases, often
simply because I have the right long distance casting
equipment, I can get a lure or bait into water that is
almost virgin territory, where the local anglers never
can, or never bother to fish. Often enough, I've found
that some streams are merely happy mediums that can be
covered by all types of gear, but never by any one type
of gear in particular. This is where a good memory of
locations and possible types of gear comes in handy.

On just about every stream I've ever fished for steelheads, sooner or later I run onto a place that is obviously
a holding spot for steelies. Normally these places are
simple to spot—you can see fish working, jumping and
sloshing around in them! Any time I see steelheads stir-
ring around that much I absolutely must stop and fish
the spot with everything I've got. I pause in my head-
long dash down the length of the stream and start trying
to figure out ways and means of getting at the fish. If
one type of lure doesn't produce, I keep switching to
others until I have either figured out the right combination or have gone through everything in the fat gear
bag I carry. And on the next trip through that area of
the stream, you can bet that I'm making tracks to get
back to this kind of place.

Often though, the day goes by without any visible
evidence that there are any fish at all in the stream. And
just as often, I find myself losing an unreasonable number of lures to hidden snags and rocks on the bottom.
This is when I bring my yarn flies into action.

The simple yarn flies have one big benefit in their
favor. They are cheap! I usually tie up my own yarn
flies, as well as my own conventional flies, so the cost
is less than 5 cents each. If I run into an area of the

stream where the snags are unreasonable, I can still go on fishing without going bankrupt. I've often found that I am fishing these areas by myself, mainly because the local fishermen have experience enough to avoid these places because of those same snags.

I would say that on average steelhead water I will cover as much as five to ten miles of new water during a full day of fishing using these methods. It's simple to see that only a day or two of this kind of fishing gives the beginner on any stream a lot of know-how that would be difficult to get any other way. I have a fairly accurate idea, after only two days or so, of just what I can expect from the type of water and the probable holds that are available, and I can make a fairly intelligent selection of tackle and methods based on this knowledge. Also, I have eliminated over 90 per cent of the water from any consideration. What you do with the other 10 per cent of good, possible water is the next important step.

As I've said before, just about every good steelhead stream in the U.S. has a road running right along the banks. But merely having that road there is not enough. It is also necessary to take the type of country into consideration. Most of the streams in the steelhead range run through pretty fierce mountain country. It does little good to know that there is a choice run or pool in a certain place if the spot is not fairly easy to get at. If it's at the bottom of a deep gorge, it's as bad as being several miles from the road. What the serious steelheader is looking for is a series of good pools or riffles that he can reasonably expect to reach during a single day's fishing, that are within a few minutes walk or climb from the road. This is what I call a "day's circuit."

On all of the rivers that I fish frequently, I have plotted out circuits. I take the type of water available and split it up into at least two separate groups; one is a fly fishing circuit and the other is a lure fishing circuit. Actually the road distance between the first pool or riffle I will fish on any given day, and the last spot may be as much as 30 to 50 miles apart. If I can reach them all in a given day's fishing it doesn't make much difference what the actual distance between them is. In fact, the farther apart they are the better chance I have to contact any migratory runs of fish that might be available in the stream; and the larger the selection of the types of water there usually is. All that remains is for me to have an accurate memory of what kind of water is located where, and to choose the right kind of tackle when I return to those spots.

Once an angler gets a few of these circuits worked out to suit himself, he can usually take steelheads pretty much at will, often far better than the local fishermen who I've noticed are prone to fish only a few favorite spots. Naturally, the ideal is to locate about a dozen good holding areas that are on level, readily accessible ground with reference to the highway. And the only way I've ever found to do this is to continue to search out new places on every successive day and on every new trip to that river. I have never found it necessary, personally, to write down the locations of particular circuits on rivers that I've fished, though some of my fishing buddies who consciously or unconsciously use the same system have a lot of off season fun fooling around with written records of their trips to these places. I have one friend who spends a good deal of time plotting his favorite spots on paper. He also carries a short bolo knife with which he trims back the brush so he can make clean backcasts to preferred lies in the stream. But this seems to me to be carrying the thing too far.

I purposely pass up places that are hard to get to on all but the rare stream. The only time I consider it necessary to climb to the bottom of a steep ravine is when the competition from other anglers makes it impossible to fish in the easily accessible places. But the competition really has to be terrific before I will sweat my way into these out of the way pools. For practical purposes, it is seldom necessary because the steelheads I've run into will show little preference to a canyon or off-road pool. After all, they will eventually have to pass through all of my favorite pools, so why bother to go through any additional trouble to get away from other anglers? Steelheading, on the vast majority of streams, is a crowded, gregarious sport. It's far better to admit this and learn to live with the problem, rather (as so many anglers try) than to spend the best part of their steelheading time trudging to off-base pools and secret places.

7 Flies for Steelheads

After a few years of fly fishing for steelheads, most anglers will have collected anywhere from a hundred fly patterns to as many as a thousand or more. It would seem that a hundred flies would be more than enough patterns for anyone to use to take a single type of fish such as the steelhead. And it is! In fact, a steelhead fisherman would be just as well off if he dropped off 96 of these patterns and merely had four.

Naturally, no ardent fly fisherman would ever be so rash as to limit himself to so few patterns. But I've found that even though the average steelheader owns several hundred flies, he rarely has a complete selection of sizes, colors, fly types, or fly weights. And the average fly box I've looked into is seriously affected by size consciousness. One fly man will be a No. 2 hook man. The next will be a No. 4 hook man, and even in the most varied box of flies I rarely see a very big spread in fly sizes. There is always a big selection of colors, though!

Of all the elements that can be varied by the fly tier to attract steelheads, color and the specific pattern used is probably the least important item. I have lost count of the number of days when I've stood in steelhead line-ups and have seen half a hundred fish landed on everything from sparkling bright patterns to dead black patterns. Yet, it is to this item of color and pattern that the average fly fisherman gives most of his attention.

The most important thing about a steelhead fly is where in the water it is fished. Usually, the deeper the fly can be worked in any given stream, the more fish it will take, regardless of size, color, and general conformation. If the average fly fisherman does nothing more than control the depth at which the fly works, he will be assured of taking many times the fish that he would if he spent his time collecting patterns.

There are several ways to make a fly sink deeply. One of the most obvious ways to get a fly to sink—and one almost completely ignored by most anglers—is to put the weight *in the hook*. By this I mean that he should select flies tied on thick wire hooks, as well as those tied on medium wire and light wire hooks. There are several dozen styles of hooks on the market. Most of the flies I've seen in tackle stores are tied on medium wire hooks, if they are tied for steelhead fishing. Most of them are tied on either the Limerick or Sproat model hooks. While these are excellent hook styles for steelheads, they are definitely not the only ones that should be used. There are extra heavy or extra strong model hooks on the market that will do a very good job of sinking a fly deep. And, there are light wire hooks, usually forged wire hooks, that will let the angler fish a fly higher up in the water for those few days when the steelheads truly "rise" to a fly.

Another way to make a fly sink deeply is to add weight *to the hook*. The first way this can be done is to use fly

tying materials that are either water absorbent or that
are themselves heavy. A fly tied with a metal, tinsel body
material, for instance, will sink deeper than one that is
tied with wool or hair as a body material. Then, the
amount of hackle and wing material can be varied to
give the fly a smaller profile that can be affected by the
current; it might sometimes be best to have extra material in the wing or body or hackle and tail of the fly.
The quickest way to get a fly to sink is to wrap fuse lead
wire around the body section of the fly, or to wrap the
fuse lead wire around the shank of the hook before the
body is tied on the fly. The newest method devised by
steelheaders to get a fly to sink deep is to tie on metal
or glass bead chain "eyes" at the head of the hook, just
behind the head of the fly. Tying on these "eyes" makes
a very attractive fly though it's doubtful whether the fish
appreciate them. In short, most of these weight adding
gimmicks are more effective ways of getting around using
split shot. I will use a split shot in my steelhead fishing,
but only as a last resort because they are devilish things
to cast (and one smack in the ear is enough to discourage
me on most days). As a tip about using split shot, I've
found it best to clamp the shot directly at the knot right
up next to the fly rather than to put it some distance up
the leader where it gives the cast a disturbing pendulum
action! I've never seen where these split shot discouraged
the steelheads from striking because they were up so close
to the fly.

After the matter of fly weight and the depth at which
the fly is fished, I consider fly size the next most important item in catching steelheads. On most days when
fish were being taken, there didn't seem to be much to
choose from in the matter of fly color. The fish didn't
seem to mind if the flies were bright or dull, but on just

about every occasion I've noticed that they would all be taken on flies that were approximately the same size.

In my own steelhead fly box I have flies that run all the way from No. 14 up to huge bucktails and streamers (which I have found very effective during deep winter fishing) that run as big as 4 in. to 6 in. in length. I will admit that most of my fish are taken on flies that run from sizes No. 8 to No. 2 but I have had many days when flies tied on comparatively small hooks or on big No. 4/0 and larger hooks produced when no other size fly would even get a bump from the fish.

As to the matter of exactly what fly patterns are best for any given situation, I've never been able to prove, to my own satisfaction, that there was much difference between them. I do believe, however, that a few general rules apply to steelhead fishing. But these are very general rules that guide my own fishing, and I do not insist that they are to be followed slavishly.

In bright or clear water, I have found that bright fly patterns produce best. In dark or discolored water, I have found that dull or dark patterns produce best for me. In the lower or tidal stretches of streams, I've found that brighter patterns, particularly those with either silver or red in them, produce best. In discolored water, large flies have proven best. In clear or bright water, small flies are best for me. But I follow these general rules very loosely. If the rule seems to be working on any given day, I follow it. If it doesn't work, I give up and try something else.

When it comes down to actually starting a fly collection for steelheads, there are certain things that the angler should keep in mind. First of all, the vast majority of flies that are associated with steelheads are tied with bucktail wings. I do not know where this all started, because a steelhead, at one time or another, will hit just about any fly ever tied to take any kind of fish. But there is a measure of logic behind the idea of making the basic fly selection around the bucktail wing flies.

The water where steelheads are normally taken is usually rather strong flowing compared to most typical trout or small-mouth bass water. This latent current power tends to plaster the hackles, wings, and other components of fly tying material down against the shank of the hook, and in general, makes any soft-tied streamer or wet fly pattern appear dead and lifeless. The common way to tie a trout wet fly is to just put a few spears of hackle on the bottom of the hook. But with most steelhead patterns I've found it best (as have the majority of experienced steelhead fishermen) to wind the hackle completely around the hook so that it flairs out and back from the hook. With a hackle wound around the hook in this way, the wing tends to hold away from the shank of the hook. Then, when the strength of the current starts working on this splayed out bucktail wing material (usually Impali), the total effect is one of life instead of lifelessness.

Probably the biggest failing in the average steelhead fly fisherman's box is that he eventually ends up with virtually nothing but bucktail (Impali) patterns. This is ridiculous when we take into consideration that the steelheads have been feeding for a period of two to four years in salt water. If anything, a bucktail pattern resembles a small bait fish more than anything else. And with a bit of imagination we could say that an orange or red wing just might resemble a shrimp; or with some extra extension, it might hint at a salmon or steelhead egg cluster. But regardless of what the bucktail looks like to the fish, it makes sense to also include a good selection of flies that have a basically different conformation or profile.

The hackle patterns, those without any wing at all, are not only easy to tie, but they are very effective, especially in the upper stretches of rivers where the fish have had a chance to get used to the food available in fresh water. The hackle flies, such as the Orleans Barber and others in the list at the back of this chapter, probably represent any number of nymph and bug life commonly found in fresh water streams. And along with the hackle patterns, the serious steelheader should consider adding buggy looking patterns from the nymph selections and such old standby flies as the Wooly Worm series. It is this idea of having a *series* of flies in a general category to offer the steelheads that seems important to me.

The streamer series of patterns have never been very prominent among steelhead fishermen in general. However, if the angler just stops to think of what the steelheads were probably feeding on when they last got a good meal in the ocean (more than likely, some form of small bait fish), it doesn't take much imagination to see that the steelheads will probably hit with relish a well tied bait fish imitation. I've found this to be the case especially where the water is very discolored as in the deep winter months of January and February. Part of this is probably due to the fact that I have become accustomed to using larger patterns that would normally be associated with salt water fly fishing during these months. And another part of it could be that the patterns in my own streamer (and large bucktail or Marabou patterns) book can simply be seen better by the fish in the low visibility of winter-swollen streams. However, I always like to have at least a fair selection of streamer patterns on hand whenever I fish for steelheads and not merely during winter. I've had some classic days fishing streamers in tide waters where the steelheads, fresh from the ocean, will land all over a fly that does a lively job of imitating a bait fish. But even if the angler does not like to use exceptionally large flies—and they can be devilish to cast in a wind—he should at least have a few patterns to try on the fish when nothing else seems to produce for him.

A type of fly that has become a must in most modern fly boxes is the Comet style of fly. In these flies (a growing series of modern flies) the tail takes the place of the wing in most patterns. As a general rule, most anglers who have a lot of steelheading experience do not really care if any given pattern has a tail or not. No angler, to my knowledge, can sustain an argument that a few spears of hackle or golden pheasant fibres could possibly make much difference to the appeal of the fly to the fish. If the fish are getting this critical, they probably wouldn't strike anything with a barb on it anyway. And the general approach to tails on steelhead flies seems to be that they sort of balance the looks of the fly from an angler's point of view —not from the fish's view of things. But the Comet and Boss series of flies make the radical departure of making the tail the biggest and most important element in the fly's makeup. It is my own guess that the steelheads look on these very swimmy patterns as a fair imitation of baby lamprey or eels and perhaps small bait fish of one kind or another. At any rate, they do give an angler an extra type of offering to present to the fish, and they are very effective. Some of the series, which like the other selections are variations on a theme, are included in the fly list at the end of the chapter along with the approved dressings.

To get back to my premise—that the place in the stream where the fly is fished is the most important single item—it won't take long for the beginner to see that he will end up with a fairly large selection of flies even if he limits himself to a maximum of perhaps six patterns.

In my own conception of steelhead fly patterns, there

are only a few kinds of flies that are necessary. They divide up naturally into (1) bright patterns, (2) dull patterns. You could add dark patterns to this if you wanted to spread the idea a bit farther.

Within the bounds of this conception as to fly color, the basic selection could be further divided up by fly types: (1) Bucktail or hair wing patterns; (2) Winged, or duck, goose quill and solid wing patterns; (3) Hackle and Nymph patterns that generally are bug imitations of one kind or another; (4) Streamer or variations on the baitfish imitation patterns; (5) the Tail patterns. And if the angler were to merely have one fly of each type in the bright and dull colors, and then to include every hook size from No. 14 up to just No. 1 in each pattern, he would end up with a tremendous and costly collection, to say the least.

If he then added only one fly of each size and of each of the bright and dull colors but tied on weighted hooks, hooks that are wrapped with fuse lead wire, heavy wire hooks, light wire hooks of various models, hooks that have bead chain "eyes" tied on them, and an extra fly or two of each type, tied with thick dressing and then tied with thinned out dressings, he would end up with a collection that added up to a total of almost a thousand flies. And this kind of selection would bring on quick bankruptcy to any angler who doesn't know how to tie up his own flies. (In fact, this was one of the big reasons that I took the time to learn how to tie my own flies long ago.)

The most logical course for the steelhead angler to take is to dump out his fly collection and finger through it before he embarks on a steelhead fly fishing trip. If the collection seems to be stunted in any size or type category, he should concentrate any money he might have available at the time, for fly buying or building, on replacing the category that seems to be lacking. For instance, several times a year I will paw through my own fly box with this in mind. Often I find that my box is heavy with bright patterns, or for that matter, with dark patterns. Again, it might be stuffed with only large flies or with small ones. Whatever the lack seems to be, I correct it before I go fishing. And being a fly tier has the added advantage of my being able to take a box of fly tying material along with me on my trips so that, should I find that the fish are partial to some specific type of pattern of fly, I can spend my evenings building up the supply of that type of pattern for the next day of fishing. However, most of my attention is directed to *where in the water the flies are going to be fished,* in other words, to the weight of the pattern and its components.

Experience over the past 20 years of fishing for steelheads has shown me conclusively that this matter of size and weight variation is the only logical approach to the subject of fishing for steelheads. After all, the steelheads, like any other fish, feed on a variety of items that they find in a variety of places in the water. If the angler limits himself any more than he has to, to a single or to a few types and sizes of flies which are fished in a limited amount of water, he is working under an unnecessary handicap. The idea of having a big spread of types, sizes, and weights on hand when the angler is actually out doing his fishing is the only solution to the problem that makes sense.

In the following lists of fly patterns I've tried to include at least a few of each basic type of fly. None of them, to me, are any more productive than others. I consider the bucktail in a bucktail wing fly the most important element in this type of fly's makeup. In the hackle pattern, the basic idea is to imitate some form of bug life, so the important elements in this kind of fly would be the relative size and color combination of all the elements. In the nymph patterns, I try to "indicate" underwater life, not to duplicate it exactly from nymphs collected from any given stream. In the streamer patterns, Marabous and combination flies, the comparatively large wing is the important thing to me. And in the Comet type of fly, the tail takes the place of the wing as the most important element.

Most of the steelhead patterns I use are tied with either wool or chenille body material. I have found that trying to tie floss body flies in the larger sizes used for steelhead fishing can become a tedious and time consuming job. I've made some experiments and I can find no indication that floss body flies produce as well or better than the easier to tie wool and chenille.

Personally I am a bug about having a fly stay together while I am fishing. Nothing gripes me more than to have a fly start to unravel when I am fishing. This predilection to built-in strength makes me lean in the direction of the fly with some kind of ribbing wrapped over the body material for added strength. If a pattern doesn't call for ribbing, I may still add some anyway. One good trick I've used frequently to get added strength into a tie is to wrap the tying thread down the length of the fly body and then back to the head again. This gives the fly a pleasing segmented look that I like. But one of the best ways to make a strong tie is to apply head cement frequently as I tie a fly. I apply at least a bit of head cement to the shank of the hook when I start a fly. This does a good job of anchoring the materials to the hook and keeps the fly from ever starting to revolve around the hook when it is given the brutal treatment of hard long line casting. A steelhead has a fair set of teeth and even the best tied flies will tend to shred when they start chomping down on them.

I have tried many times to get some kind of rule to

guide me in basic fly color selection. I've never been able to do any more than sort of hint at what *seems* to be best. The flies with red in them appear to be a primary color requirement in any complete fly box. But including plenty of yellows, whites, and oranges are a must for me. Too, I wouldn't be found dead on any steelhead stream without plenty of blacks, grays, and browns. In short, just pick some of each. . . .

These BUCKTAIL or WINGED patterns are all tied with rooster hackle in my own book. I like the way the stiff rooster hackle holds the wing away from the body material. I have made experiments with conventional wet fly ties where the hackle was tied only on the under side of the fly, and they proved to be far less effective than those tied completely around the hook. Too, I've found it a fairly good trick to tie a few hackles *in front of the wing on a few flies,* though I can't say that this is essential to any marked extent. Too, in all of the series, I tie some flies in the "low water" style of a small fly being tied on a big hook; it makes them sink well.

ADMIRAL. Body: red wool. Tail: red bucktail, short. Ribbing: gold tinsel. Hackle: red. Wing: white polar bear.

ALASKA MARY ANN. Body: white chenille. Tag: silver. Tail: red hackle. Wing: white polar bear, jungle cock overlay.

ALDER. Body: olive chenille. Hackle: blue or black. Wing: brown and black bucktail, mixed.

BISHOP. Body: silver tinsel. Hackle: brown. Wing: brown bucktail.

BLACK COACHMAN. Body: black chenille. Hackle: brown. Wing: white bucktail.

BLACK DEMON. Body: gold. Tail: golden pheasant. Hackle: orange. Wing: black bucktail, jungle cock.

BLACK GNAT BUCKTAIL. Body: black chenille. Tail: red. Hackle: black. Wing: brown bucktail.

BLACK JOE. Body: black chenille. Tag: red silk. Tail: red hackle. Hackle: black. Wing: scarlet with white.

BLACK PRINCE. Body: black wool or chenille. Tail: red. Ribbing: silver tinsel. Hackle: black. Wing: brown.

BLUE BOTTLE. Body: gray wool. Tail: black hackle. Hackle: black. Wing: gray squirrel.

BROWN MALLARD. Body: yellow wool. Tail: brown mallard. Ribbing: gold tinsel. Tag: gold tinsel. Hackle: brown. Wing: brown mallard.

CANADA. Body: red wool or spun fur. Tail: red wool, picked with needle. Ribbing: gold tinsel. Hackle: orange. Wing: turkey spears.

CARSON. Body: peacock hurl, wind band of red silk. Tail: golden pheasant tippet. Hackle: brown. Wing: red and white impali, jungle cock overlay.

CHAMBERS. Body: red wool. Tail: yellow bucktail, short. Hackle: brown. Wing: mottled turkey, divided.

CINNAMON. Body: brown wool. Ribbing: gold tinsel. Hackle: brown. Wing: brown bucktail, jungle cock.

COACHMAN BUCKTAIL. Body: peacock. Tail: red. Hackle: brown. Wing: white bucktail, jungle cock.

CONCH. Body: olive wool. Tail: red goose quill fibres. Hackle: green or gray. Wing: peacock hurl, bunched, divided.

CUMMING'S. Body: yellow and red, one half. Ribbing: gold tinsel. Hackle: red. Wing: brown bucktail, jungle cock overlay.

DEACON. Body: yellow wool. Hackle: yellow, palmered, red at front. Wing: mallard flank, divided, jungle cock.

DEER FLY. Body: spun fur, gray. Hackle: gray. Wing: gray bucktail and gray hackle tips.

DIXIE. Body: gold tinsel. Tail: yellow hackle. Hackle: red. Wing: white.

DODGER. Body: brown wool. Ribbing: gold tinsel. Hackle: red. Wing: pheasant tail fibres.

DOLLY VARDEN. Body: white wool. Tail: brown hackle. Ribbing: brown wool, thick. Hackle: brown. Wing: gray squirrel, jungle cock.

DOSE. Body: black wool. Tail: yellow quill, goose. Ribbing: gold tinsel. Tag: gold tinsel—both sides of tail. Hackle: dun or coot. Wing: pheasant tail, jungle cock.

DUGMORE. Body: black wool. Ribbing: silver tinsel. Hackle: black. Wing: gray squirrel.

DUSTY MILLER. Body: silver tinsel. Tag: silver. Tail: red hackle. Hackle: guinea. Wing: brown turkey, mottled.

EEL OPTIC. Body: silver tinsel, oval. Wing: red bucktail. Head: very large painted white with eyes of red and black. (White paint and eyes optional.)

EMERALD. Body: green chenille. Tail: yellow hackle tip. Ribbing: gold tinsel. Hackle: brown. Wing: coot fibres.

FALL FAVORITE. Body: silver tinsel. Hackle: red. Wing: orange.

FERN. Body: silver tinsel. Hackle: dark brown. Wing: polar bear.

FISHER. Body: yellow wool. Tail: mandarin. Ribbing: gold tinsel. Hackle: red. Wing: white bucktail overlay of black bucktail, jungle cock.

FLIGHT'S FANCY. Body: yellow wool. Tail: brown hackle. Ribbing: gold tinsel. Hackle: brown. Wing: white goose, divided, jungle cock.

FOX. Body: gold tinsel. Tail: brown hackle. Hackle: brown. Wing: white bucktail.

GIBSON GIRL. Body: orange wool. Ribbing: gold tinsel. Tag: gold tinsel. Tail: golden pheasant. Hackle: brown. Wing: brown bucktail.

GOLD HILTON. Body: black chenille. Tail: gray hackle fibres. Ribbing: gold tinsel. Hackle: brown. Wing: mallard flank, divided, short.

GOLDEN DEMON. Body: flat gold. Tail: golden pheasant. Hackle: orange. Wing: brown mallard, jungle cock overlay.

GOLDEN PHEASANT. Body: red wool. Tail: black hackle. Ribbing: gold tinsel. Hackle: red. Wing: golden pheasant.

GORDON. Body: yellow wool. Tail: mallard, yellow. Ribbing: gold tinsel. Hackle: badger. Wing: mallard, yellow, divided.

GRAY DRAKE. Body: white wool. Tail: mallard flank. Ribbing: black wool. Hackle: gray. Wing: mallard.

GRAY JAY. Body: gray wool. Tail: golden pheasant. Ribbing: silver tinsel. Hackle: brown. Wing: blue jay, divided.

GREEN DRAKE. Body: yellow wool. Tail: mixed green and yellow hackle. Ribbing: gold tinsel. Hackle: green. Wing: mallard, yellow.

HAWK. Body: spun fur. Tail: brown, mottled turkey. Ribbing: black wool. Hackle: brown. Wing: brown turkey, divided, jungle cock.

HOOKER. Body: yellow wool. Ribbing: black wool. Hackle: brown. Wing: black bucktail.

IRISH TURKEY. Body: green wool. Tail: yellow hackle. Ribbing: gold tinsel. Hackle: brown. Wing: turkey, brown, mottled.

JOCK SCOTT. Body: yellow silk, rear half; black silk, front half; silver rib over. Tail: golden pheasant. Hackle: guinea. Wing: brown mallard with peacock sword, jungle cock overlay.

JUNE BLACK. Body: red wool. Ribbing: silver tinsel. Tag: silver tinsel. Hackle: black. Wing: brown turkey.

KATE. Body: red wool. Ribbing: gold tinsel. Tag: gold

tinsel. Tail: golden pheasant. Hackle: yellow. Wing: red, yellow and blue mallard or bucktail; jungle cock.

KING FISHER. Body: red wool. Tail: golden pheasant. Ribbing: gold tinsel. Hackle: brown. Wing: teal flank, jungle cock.

LARAMIE. Body: red wool. Tail: red goose. Ribbing: silver tinsel. Tag: silver tinsel. Hackle: black. Wing: gray bucktail, jungle cock.

LIGHT EDSON TIGER. Body: peacock herl. Tail: red hackle. Hackle: red. Wing: yellow bucktail.

MAJOR. Body: brown fur, spun. Tail: red and yellow bucktail. Ribbing: gold tinsel. Tag: gold tinsel. Hackle: brown. Wing: yellow and red, overlay yellow bucktail.

MALLARD. Body: gray wool. Tail: mallard flank. Hackle: brown. Wing: mallard flank, short, divided.

MARCH BROWN EAST. Body: brown wool. Ribbing: gold. Tail: red hackle. Hackle: brown and grizzly. Wing: brown with jungle cock overlay.

MARCH BROWN WEST. Body: spun brown fur. Tail: partridge. Ribbing: gold. Hackle: partridge. Wing: pheasant, divided.

MARCH DUN. Body: olive chenille. Tag: yellow wool. Wing: gray mallard.

MC GINTY. Body: yellow and black chenille. Tail: red hackle and teal. Hackle: brown. Wing: brown bucktail overlaid with white bucktail.

MC KENZIE. Body: green wool. Tail: brown hackle. Ribbing: gold tinsel. Hackle: brown. Wing: gray squirrel.

MICKEY FINN. Body: silver tinsel. Wing: red and yellow bucktail layered, jungle cock.

MINNOW, GOLD. Body: gold tinsel. Hackle: red and green, mixed. Wing: white bucktail, orange hackle tips, overlay of gray bucktail.

MONTREAL. Body: red wool. Tail: red hackle. Ribbing: gold tinsel. Tag: gold tinsel. Hackle: red. Wing: turkey divided.

MOTH. Body: spun brown fur. Ribbing: gold tinsel. Tag: gold tinsel. Hackle: brown. Wing: brown bucktail.

OAK. Body: orange wool. Tail: brown turkey. Hackle: brown. Wing: brown turkey.

ORANGE BLACK. Body: orange wool. Tail: black hackle. Ribbing: black wool. Hackle: black. Wing: black bucktail.

PALE DUN. Body: yellow wool. Tail: teal. Ribbing: gold. Hackle: coot. Wing: gray bucktail.

PARMACHENE BELLE. Body: yellow. Ribbing: silver. Tail: red and white hackle. Hackle: scarlet and white blended. Wing: white bucktail with red goose overlay.

PIKER. Body: orange wool. Tag: gold tinsel. Hackle: brown. Wing: white goose.

PLATH. Body: blue wool. Tail: red hackle. Hackle: red. Wing: gray squirrel.

POLAR SHRIMP. Body: orange wool. Tail: red hackle. Hackle: orange. Wing: white polar bear, tied down rear.

POORMAN. Body: brown fur, spun. Tag: gold tinsel. Hackle: brown. Wing: pheasant.

POTTER. Body: blue wool, light. Ribbing: black wool. Hackle: brown. Wing: gray bucktail.

QUAKER. Body: gray wool. Tail: mallard flank. Ribbing: gold tinsel. Tag: gold tinsel. Hackle: pun. Wing: gray squirrel.

RAILBIRD. Body: red wool palmered with red hackle. Tail: red hackle. Hackle: yellow. Wing: black and white teal.

RED ASH. Body: red wool. Ribbing: gold tinsel. Tag: gold tinsel. Hackle: dun or coot. Wing: mallard, brown.

RIO GRANDE KING. Body: black chenille. Tail: yellow hackle. Tag: gold wool. Hackle: brown. Wing: white bucktail.

SAND FLY. Body: blue wool. Tail: dun hackle. Tag: silver tinsel. Hackle: brown. Wing: mottled brown turkey.

SCARLET IBIS. Body: red wool. Tail: red goose. Ribbing: gold tinsel. Hackle: red. Wing: red goose.

SETH GREEN. Body: green wool. Ribbing: yellow wool. Hackle: brown. Wing: mottled turkey.

SHRIMP, ORANGE. Body: spun fur, brown. Tail: golden pheasant. Ribbing: silver tinsel. Hackle: orange. Wing: orange bucktail, jungle cock.

SILVER DEMON. Body: silver tinsel. Tag: silver tinsel. Tail: orange hackle. Hackle: orange. Wing: gray mallard flank.

SILVER DOCTOR. Body: silver tinsel. Tail: red hackle, golden pheasant crest. Hackle: blue overlaid with guinea. Wing: brown peacock swords on sides.

SILVER GHOST. Body: green chenille. Tail: mandarin. Hackle: badger. Wing: gray squirrel.

SILVER HILTON. Body: black chenille. Tail: mallard flank. Ribbing: silver tinsel. Hackle: gray. Wing: gray hackle tips, short.

SOCK. Body: yellow wool. Hackle: black. Wing: black bucktail.

SUPERVISOR. Body: flat silver tinsel. Tail: red wool. Hackle: red. Wing: blue and olive overlay, white and red.

TETON. Body: yellow wool. Tail: brown hackle. Ribbing: gold tinsel. Tag: gold tinsel. Hackle: brown. Wing: gray bucktail, jungle cock.

THOR. Body: red chenille. Tail: orange. Hackle: brown. Wing: white bucktail.

THUNDER. Body: black wool. Tail: yellow hackle tip, flat. Ribbing: red wool. Hackle: yellow. Wing: guinea.

UMPQUA. Body: yellow wool, rear third; red chenille. Ribbing: silver tinsel. Tail: white bucktail. Hackle: brown. Wing: white bucktail red bucktail overlay, each side.

VAN LUEVEN. Body: red wool. Tail: red bucktail, short. Hackle: brown. Wing: white bucktail.

VICTORIA. Body: green wool. Tail: golden pheasant. Ribbing: gold tinsel. Tag: gold tinsel. Hackle: yellow. Wing: brown mottled turkey, jungle cock.

VOLUNTEER. Body: yellow wool. Tail: red hackle. Ribbing: gold tinsel. Tag: gold tinsel. Hackle: green. Wing: golden pheasant.

WARWICK. Body: green chenille. Tail: red goose. Hackle: red. Wing: peacock hurl.

WELL'S SPECIAL. Body: rear, silver tinsel; forward, peacock hurl. Tail: red. Hackle: yellow. Wing: teal, overlaid brown, scarlet and blue, jungle cock overlay.

WINTERS. Body: red wool. Tail: brown mallard. Hackle: dun or black. Wing: brown mallard.

YELLOW JAY. Body: yellow wool. Tail: yellow hackle. Hackle: yellow. Wing: blue jay, divided.

YELLOW SPINNER. Body: yellow chenille. Tail: yellow hackle. Hackle: red. Wing: blue goose.

In the STREAMER selection I feel that the important item is for the angler to sort of let himself go. The streamers are more or less of an added attraction to the fly box. Their basic function is to give the angler one more thing to offer the fish. I have relatively few small streamers in my fly boxes because there is little that the small streamer can do that the bucktail or hackle patterns can't do just as well. My own streamer selection has little rime or reason, and some of the patterns are rather frightening to look at because they are so huge and garish.

BLACK GHOST. Body: black wool. Tail: golden pheasant.

Ribbing: silver tinsel. Hackle: golden pheasant, under only. Wing: white hackle feathers, jungle cock.

BLACK MARABOU. Body: black chenille. Ribbing: fluorescent red wool. Tag: fluorescent red wool, wide. Hackle: orange, under only. Wing: black marabou thinly tied.

BLUE DEVIL. Body: gold tinsel. Tail: golden pheasant. Hackle: gray with golden pheasant under. Wing: gray hackle feather, jungle cock.

GOLD. Body: gold tinsel. Tail: golden pheasant. Hackle: red. Wing: white bucktail under brown.

GRAY GHOST. Body: orange wool. Ribbing: silver tinsel. Hackle: peacock hurl, under only, long with white bucktail. Wing: gray hackle feathers, golden pheasant cheek, jungle cock eye.

JERSEY MINNOW. Body: gold tinsel. Tail: golden pheasant. Hackle: brown and pink, mixed. Wing: badger hackle feathers.

NEEDABEH. Body: red wool. Ribbing: silver tinsel. Tag: silver tinsel. Hackle: yellow and red mixed. Wing: yellow feathers inside orange, jungle cock.

OPTIC BUCKTAIL. Body: silver tinsel, flat. Tail: red hackle. Ribbing: silver tinsel, oval. Wing: white bucktail under black, jungle cock. Head: twice normal size, white eye with black pupil.

SCOTT. Body: brown wool. Tail: red hackle. Ribbing: silver tinsel. Tag: silver tinsel. Hackle: yellow. Wing: yellow bucktail, jungle cock.

TRINITY. Body: red wool. Tail: teal flank. Ribbing: silver tinsel. Tag: silver tinsel. Hackle: red. Wing: gray hackle feathers, jungle cock.

WESLEY. Body: silver tinsel flat. Tail: golden pheasant. Ribbing: silver tinsel, oval. Hackle: black. Wing: white bucktail under gray, jungle cock.

WHITE MARABOU. Body: silver tinsel. Hackle: red, under only. Wing: white marabou, peacock overlay.

YELLOW MARABOU. Body: silver tinsel. Hackle: red outside of wing. Wing: yellow marabou, peacock overlay.

In this selection of HACKLE patterns, I usually tie my own flies with limp hen hackle instead of the stiffer rooster hackle that is commonly associated with dry fly patterns. In all of these patterns, ribbing is a matter of personal taste as far as I am concerned. If the tier is interested in having stronger flies he can rib them with any material he likes. The general idea is to end up with either a bright or a dull pattern, not to be meticulous about the exact materials used in any given tie. For instance, there really isn't much practical difference between materials like mallard flank and teal flank feathers. One will do as well as the other. And a dark brown hackle feather is just as effective as a light brown hackle feather.

BROWN HACKLE. Body: olive wool. Tail: brown hackle. Ribbing: silver tinsel. Tag: silver tinsel. Hackle: brown.

BUTCHER. Body: red wool. Tail: red goose quill. Ribbing: gold tinsel. Hackle: badger.

BUZZ. Body: green chenille. Tag: yellow wool. Hackle: brown.

CAHILL. Body: gray wool. Tail: teal flank, yellow. Hackle: brown. Wing: teal flank, yellow, jungle cock.

GOLDEN ROD. Body: red floss, padded. Tail: red goose. Tag: green chenille. Ribbing: gold tinsel. Hackle: orange. Wing: jungle cock, divided.

GRAY HACKLE YELLOW. Body: yellow floss. Ribbing: gold tinsel. Tag: gold tinsel. Tail: red. Hackle: gray. Wing: jungle cock.

GREEN MIDGE. Body: green wool. Tag: gold tinsel. Ribbing: gold tinsel. Hackle: white.

GRIZZLY PALMER. Body: yellow wool. Tail: red. Hackle: gray, palmered.

IMP. Body: black wool. Tail: red hackle. Hackle: black, full.

MARLOW. Body: red wool. Tag: gold tinsel. Ribbing: gold tinsel. Hackle: badger.

MIDGE BLACK. Body: gray wool. Hackle: dun.

ORLEANS BARBER. Body: red chenille. Tail: wood duck. Hackle: gray.

PRIEST. Body: gray spun fur. Tail: red hackle. Hackle: badger.

SPIDER. Body: red wool, padded. Tail: red goose quill. Ribbing: gold tinsel. Hackle: grouse.

WHITE HACKLE. Body: white wool. Ribbing: black wool. Hackle: white.

These NYMPH patterns are tied fairly close to the original patterns. I stick to the basic tie that made them productive because I feel that using them is a specialized thing. I rarely use them when I am searching for fish because I feel that the common hackle patterns will do as good a job as the nymph patterns will. I normally use them when I feel that the fishing is of a critical nature, as in low water fishing during the summer and early fall, or whenever the water is very clear. In short, if the pattern calls for spun animal fur of a certain kind, I feel that I am not doing the pattern justice if I do not use that kind of material. If the fishing isn't critical, why use nymphs?

BLACK NYMPH. Body: black chenille. Tail: brown hackle. Ribbing: gold tinsel, thin. Hackle: black, sides only.

BLUE NYMPH. Body: blue chenille. Tail: mallard flank. Ribbing: gold tinsel, thin oval. Hackle: mallard flank, feelers.

BROWN AND WHITE NYMPH. Body: white wool, brown

chenille laid over top. Tail: black hackle. Ribbing: black tying thread. Hackle: black, below only.

BUG NYMPH. Body: black chenille. Hackle: coot flank, rear and front at sides only.

CADDIS. Body: gray chenille. Tail: 3 peacock hurls. Ribbing: black tying thread. Hackle: peacock hurl feelers.

FREEMAN SHRIMP. Body: fluorescent wool. Ribbing: silver tinsel. Hackle: orange, palmered, cut off flush on top. Wing: orange bucktail, tied down at rear of body.

FUR NYMPH. Body: spun animal fur, brown. Tail: teal flank. Ribbing: black tying thread. Hackle: teal flank, sides only.

GOLDEN BUG NYMPH. Body: rear, gold tinsel, oval; front black wool. Tail: peacock hurl. Hackle: peacock hurl, sides only.

GRAY AND BROWN NYMPH. Body: gray wool, brown chenille top of back. Tail: brown hackle. Ribbing: black tying thread. Hackle: brown hackle feelers.

GRAY BUG. Body: gray animal fur, spun. Tail: gray hackle tip, short. Ribbing: black tying thread. Hackle: gray, below only. Wing: short gray hackle tips tied back.

GRAY NYMPH. Body: spun animal fur, gray. Tail: mallard flank. Ribbing: small gold tinsel. Hackle: mallard flank feelers.

OLIVE NYMPH. Body: olive green wool. Tail: teal flank. Ribbing: black tying thread. Hackle: teal flank feelers.

RED NYMPH. Body: peacock hurl front, red wool rear. Tail: guinea. Ribbing: black tying thread. Hackle: guinea feelers.

RUST NYMPH. Body: rust brown, red wool, picked out. Tail: guinea. Ribbing: yellow wool. Hackle: guinea, feelers, skimpy.

WOOLY WORM. Body: black chenille. Tail: gray hackle tip. Ribbing: gold tinsel. Hackle: gray palmered.

Note: I use Wooly Worm patterns in several color combinations. The best are dull: browns, grays and blues, and those tied with skimpy hen hackle work best for me.

YELLOW AND BROWN NYMPH. Body: yellow wool, brown chenille up. Tail: black hackle. Ribbing: black tying thread. Hackle: brown, below only.

These COMET type patterns are really a variation on the basic theme that the fly should be swimmy. I tend to prefer the flies that are tied with tail material that is rather limp in general makeup. But if a fly calls for a certain type of material such as Impali, I would still consider the pattern productive and it should be called by the same name if the materials used were bucktail, polar bear, or marabou, just as long as the material was the same color as indicated in the pattern list. In fact, if the angler merely took any pattern from the bucktail fly list and just transferred the wing to the tail section, I can't see anything wrong with the method. I like my Comet patterns to have tails about 1½ times the length of the hook shank. I have never seen where steelheads struck "short" and have never bothered with trailer hooks.

Boss. Body: black chenille. Tail: black bucktail. Ribbing: silver tinsel. Hackle: red.

Boss, BLUE. Body: blue chenille. Tail: polar bear and white marabou, mixed. Ribbing: silver tinsel. Hackle: white.

Boss, GRAY. Body: olive chenille. Tail: gray squirrel. Ribbing: silver tinsel. Hackle: red.

Boss, ORANGE. Body: orange chenille. Tail: orange marabou. Ribbing: silver tinsel. Hackle: red.

Boss, RED. Body: red chenille. Tail: red bucktail. Ribbing: silver tinsel. Hackle: black.

Boss, WHITE. Body: white chenille. Tail: white marabou. Ribbing: black wool. Hackle: black.

Boss, Yellow. Body: yellow chenille. Tail: yellow marabou. Ribbing: gold tinsel. Hackle: yellow.

Comet. Body: yellow wool. Tail: yellow impali. Ribbing: gold tinsel. Hackle: yellow.

Comet, Black. Body: black wool. Tail: black bucktail. Ribbing: gold tinsel. Hackle: black.

Comet, Blue. Body: blue wool. Tail: white polar bear. Ribbing: gold tinsel. Hackle: white.

Comet, Brown. Body: brown wool. Tail: brown bucktail. Ribbing: silver tinsel. Hackle: brown.

Comet, Gray. Body: gray wool. Tail: gray squirrel. Ribbing: silver tinsel. Hackle: red.

Comet, Olive. Body: olive wool. Tail: black marabou. Ribbing: silver tinsel. Hackle: red.

Comet, Orange. Body: fluorescent orange wool. Tail: orange impali. Ribbing: gold tinsel. Hackle: black.

Comet, Red. Body: red wool. Tail: red impali. Ribbing: silver tinsel. Hackle: brown.

Comet, Yellow. Body: gold wool. Tail: yellow marabou. Ribbing: gold tinsel. Hackle: yellow.

Rat-tail. Body: orange chenille. Hackle: orange, under only. Wing: black bucktail, long, tied down at rear of body, to extend twice length of body.

Note: This pattern can be tied with any color combination. Best for me has been dark upper and light under. Any wing pattern can be used by merely using a long wing and tying down at rear of body.

Razor Back. Body: orange wool, black chenille along top of back. Tail: orange bucktail under black. Ribbing: silver tinsel. Hackle: red.

Razor Back, Marabou. Body: white wool, black chenille along top of back. Tail: white marabou under black bucktail. Ribbing: silver tinsel. Hackle: black.

Razor Back, White. Body: white wool, black chenille

along top of back. Tail: white bucktail under black. Ribbing: silver tinsel. Hackle: black.

RAZOR BACK, YELLOW. Body: yellow wool, olive chenille along top of back. Tail: yellow bucktail under peacock hurl. Ribbing: gold tinsel. Hackle: yellow.

YARN FLY. Double point hooks. Body: fluorescent red wool. Hackle: fluorescent red wool tide streamer.

Note: This pattern, if it can be called that, can be tied with any kind and color of wool. I have had my best luck with those tied of angora wool in bright, fluorescent colors, primarily reds and oranges.

8 Summer and Fall Steelheads

Most of the steelhead streams that have become world famous are those that have been blessed with a summer or early fall run of steelies. Another noticeable thing about "famous" steelhead streams in general is that they all have fairly good access. But exactly why it is that one specific stream in a given area, where there may well be several other streams with the same characteristics, will support a good run of these maverick summer run steelheads is still a mystery to scientists and fishermen alike.

This matter of different strains of steelheads, which habitually migrate at odd times of the year, is just another of the discoveries that must await the maturity of the science of ichthyology. But the angler is merely interested in the basic information about which of the many hundreds of possible streams on the Pacific coast offers him the best chance to get himself into a run of steelheads during the summer and fall months.

I'll start off with an assumption that, at the present time, is neither provable nor unprovable: It is very, very likely that every single stream in the entire Pacific coast drainage, that does not close up at the mouth of the stream during the summer and fall low-water months, has a run of steelheads, however small that run might be. It is also possible to assume that only those streams that have a fairly large number of these maverick steelheads running into them during the summer and fall months are worth the angler's notice. Also, it makes little sense, for the purposes of this book, to mention streams that are so far off the beaten path that they are all but impossible to reach.

I feel that this matter of accessibility is almost as important as the fact of whether or not a river we are considering has any kind of summer run worth noting. In this way we can automatically drop from consideration all of the hundreds of streams, like those along the remote stretches of Alaska and the British Columbian coasts. I have no doubts that there are many streams in both of these areas that support good or even spectacular runs of summer steelheads; but of what possible value are they to us, as anglers, if we cannot readily reach them?

While we are considering accessibility, I'd like to point out a fact about the newest "famous" river, British Columbia's Kispiox River. About a decade or so back, the road access was greatly improved to Hazelton, B. C. And once this road was reasonably passable to the average guy, there started a trickle of information which soon became an avalanche of statistics about huge steelheads which has all added up to make the Kispiox the most desirable steelhead river in the world. The current world record fish came out of the Kispiox, *but not until a large number of anglers were given reasonable access.*

It's practical to assume that the Kispiox has held large numbers of huge fish for thousands of years. But until the fishermen could get to them, they were of little value to anyone.

With a few exceptions, all of the famous summer run steelhead streams have much larger runs of much larger fish during the winter months. This is an important point to remember, because so many anglers fail to realize that a river that is considered good and which has been made famous because so many people can fish it during balmy weather is just as good, and probably better, after the rains of winter have opened it up to the larger fish.

It is relatively easy to name the few streams in the whole range of the steelheads which have summer and fall runs of fish that are large enough to be worth the attention of the average fisherman. California has the great Klamath River in the far northern part of the state near the Oregon-California border. The Klamath is actually an entire drainage system composed of half a dozen major streams. But only the Trinity, Salmon, and Scott Rivers are of importance to the angler who wants to fish in this area. The main Klamath River itself absorbs by far the majority of the angling attention that is given to this drainage. And the first 20 miles of stream up from the mouth of the Klamath supports a good 90 per cent of the fishing in the Klamath River drainage.

Taking only the Klamath as a basic example, the beginner has to realize that if I say that fishing is at its peak in the Klamath River during the middle part of September during most years, what I actually mean is that the hordes of anglers from all over the world who fish the first few miles of the stream are catching most of their fish during this period. The important point I am trying to make is that the angler who wants to really get into the choice fishing in the Klamath River drainage should remember that the fish are still moving upstream at a fairly steady pace after this so-called peak of action at the mouth of the stream. I maintain that the most pleasant, and usually the most productive, fishing for any single angler or small group will come if the fishing is done well away from these crowded areas.

This type of reasoning applies to every "famous" steelhead stream. The Rogue and the North Fork of the Umpqua are just two more examples of this same kind of mass interest phenomenon. And even the comparatively remote Kispiox River comes under the same set of logical rules.

In the case of the Kispiox, the area of the stream that gets 90 per cent of the angling attention is that immediately available to anglers who headquarter in the town of Hazelton in spite of the fact that the Kispiox is merely another type of stream system or drainage—just like the Klamath. Most of the other streams in the immediate area are fairly accessible, such as the Bulkley which provides exceptional sport out of Smithers.

Another good example of fishing summer and fall run streams is the situation found in the Victoria area on Vancouver Island. On Vancouver Island, if you should ask any of the local sporting goods dealers or fish and game men where you should look for steelheads during the summer and early fall months, they will tell you that the west coast streams are the summer streams and the east coast streams are the winter run streams. No matter whom you ask, this answer will be the same.

But when you actually fish Vancouver Island for a few seasons you will find that this is an extremely vague approach to finding summer run—or for that matter winter run—fishing. Actually, Vancouver Island is the classic example of the steelhead fishing problem.

Victoria, located at the southeast corner of the island, and Nanaimo, about an hour's drive north on the east coast, are the usual jump-off points for anglers. The natives consider all of the streams to the west of Victoria as their summer run fishing spots, and they will completely avoid becoming involved with any kind of suggestion that you just might find some fair to good fishing as far north on the east coast as the Campbell River. And yet, if you were to go north as far as the Campbell River, and even 50 miles beyond, to the point where the paved roads peter out completely, you would have invested as little as half a day of your precious time in the entire project of checking out all of the many rivers that just might possibly have a fair run of fish in them at the time you are there—regardless of what time of year this happens to be.

When your host or adviser on Vancouver Island says that the streams such as the Jordan, San Juan, Harris Creek, Ash, and Stamp Rivers are your best bets for summer run fish, you should believe him. But it is also true that most of the other rivers on the west coast may be just as good, if not better, than those named; but they are much harder to get to. If you should fail to score in these preferred streams you should definitely not throw in the sponge and quit. As long as you are in the area it certainly makes sense for you to also try the fishing in at least a selection of these other east coast streams. The object here is that the angler new to the island has invested a good deal of time in merely getting into the area and he should hedge his bet by fishing other readily available streams, just as long as he does not have to spend too much time doing a fair job of the whole project.

Just the opposite set of conditions is faced on the British Columbia mainland. The Thompson River, about 250 miles from Vancouver City on Highway 1 (Trans-Canada), is a classic example of the cul de sac that many beginning anglers may find themselves in. When you look at a road map of British Columbia it looks like the Thompson River is extremely accessible. The main highway, No. 1, the best road in the province, is shown running right along next to the river. But when you actually get to the area you will discover that the major part of the river is at the bottom of an impossible canyon. There is a short stretch of the whole Thompson River in the Spence's Bridge area of about 15 miles at the most which can be reached at all by the angler. Also, the fishable stretch of the Thompson River is within a five or six hour drive of Seattle, Washington, and Vancouver, British Columbia, so the few miles of water which is fishable at all will have to support an almost unbelievable amount of angling pressure.

This is not to say that the Thompson River is not an exceptional steelhead stream. Just the opposite is true. The Thompson River is unique in that it drains the high mountain area to the east and is located, here in the lower stretches, in what is known as "the dry belt" of British Columbia. This combination of being a fair distance from the rushing mountain streams and running for a great distance below Kamloops Lake which settles any silt makes for extremely clear, cold water that is ideal for steelhead fishing. The Thompson is also a fairly large river that tempts a great percentage of the larger fish from the entire Frazer River system. And the average fish that is caught in this stream will go 17 lbs.—a handsome average for any stream.

The reason I say that a river such as the Thompson is

a cul de sac for the beginner is that it is all alone. The nearest other stream that is valuable at all for steelhead fishing is the Kispiox which is about a two day drive from the fishable portion of the Thompson. In other words, if you don't manage to find a run of fish in the limited stretch of the Thompson that you can fish, you are forced to drive about 600 miles just to try your hand at another stream—which also might not have a run of summer fish in it at that specific time. The better strategy would be to head straight for the Skeena-Kispiox-Bulkley drainage in the first place and then return for a fast shot at fishing the Thompson if you get skunked on these others. Also, as a general rule, the Kispiox-Bulkley systems will have fish in them from August until late spring, while the Thompson is normally considered best from very late October until spring.

So far in this chapter on summer fishing for steelies I have tried to give a general picture of how the angler should consider all of the elements of a stream system rather than to merely pick a given stream with a good record for past performance and bet all his chips on that single piece of water. I have purposely bypassed other reasonably productive summer and fall run streams such as the Eel in California and the Kalama, Wind, and Washougal in Washington. These streams are so difficult for the beginner or the outsider to fish that they might be best stricken from the list of good summer run possibilities.

For instance, the Eel River built up its summer run reputation almost a half century ago. But since that time there have been vast changes in the entire watershed of this extensive stream. The Eel River is one of the few streams in the North American continent which flows in a northerly direction. It drains several mountain ranges. These mountain ranges were once completely covered with dense stands of timber from gigantic pine forests to the monolithic redwood rain forests. These forests have been all but denuded, and the once mighty Eel River is a mere shadow of its former self. The rains that pelt this area of the Pacific Coast come gushing down the bare mountains and flood the Eel at the slightest hint of volume. Then they dry out quickly and the Eel returns to a status of not much more than a fair sized creek. What all this adds up to, from an angling standpoint, is that the steelheads are usually stuck in the tidal stretch of the river during the late summer and early fall months. This tidal stretch of the Eel is limited to the stream below the town of Fortuna. While this is some of the finest fly fishing water in the world, the actual area suitable for comfortable, productive angling is only a few miles long. And in the average year only the local anglers are handy during the latter part of September and the month of October to sample the runs of smallish steeelheads that attend to the memory of this raped stream. Hence, it is only of passing interest to the angler who is serious about his steelheading.

The Washington streams like the Wind, Washougal, and Kalama are small streams that are more or less limited to local angler attention. The best months on these streams are October and part of September during reasonably wet years when the flow is at least moderate. The way I personally go about fishing these streams is more a matter of proximity than of making a long trip to take a crack at them. If I happen to be going through the area during the select months, I take a look at the weather, and if it has been reasonably mild, I stop for a day or so to fish. If there has been a measurable amount of rain in the past few weeks or if the region is in the grips of any kind of a drought, I pass it up for greener pastures.

Here are my own personal preferences for times of year and the order of preference that I would fish the key streams: During the months of August and September I would like to be on the Kispiox-Bulkley circuit in British Columbia. A second choice at this time would be the west coast Vancouver Island streams with enough time to try some of the east coast streams. A third choice would be the Lower Klamath River and I'd like to have a boat so that I could go upstream to get away from the big crowds. A fourth choice for August and September fishing would be Gold Beach on the Rogue River. You'll catch more salmon in the Rogue nowadays than you will steelheads, though.

For October to November fishing my first choice would be the middle Klamath River and the lower Trinity River in California near the tiny hamlet of Weitchpec, the junction of the two rivers. The second choice would be the Thompson but preferably in the latter part of November in the Spence's Bridge area. Third choice would be the Vancouver Island streams—I'd want to be able to fish all of them, though. And last choice is a tossup between the lower Eel, the Rogue in Oregon, and the Wind-Washougal-Kalama in Washington State.

I have said nothing about the techniques that I would use for fishing summer and fall run steelheads. I did this on purpose because I consider all summer and fall fishing as special and finicky fishing for steelheads. I'll have more to say about these techniques in the chapters on special techniques, but in general, summer steelhead fishing is done just about the same as the fisherman would angle for larger trouts in large streams anywhere in the country. In short, any good book on trout angling technique would prepare the angler for summer run steelhead fishing.

9 Winter Steelhead Fishing

When an angler says that he is going winter steelhead fishing he usually means that he plans his sport during the months from December through February. And these months actually are the heart of the winter steelhead season throughout the range of the species. However, for our purposes here I'd like to make the specific point that the term "winter steelhead fishing" should actually refer to a set of conditions rather than a specific time of the year.

I have lived and fished on the Pacific coast all of my life and I've come to the conclusion that winter conditions can settle in any time from late September on, or it can hold off and not actually arrive until sometime in February. So, if the rains which swell the streams come early in the season, say in late September or early October, the steelheads usually will arrive early that year. By the same token, if the rains of winter do not arrive until after New Year's Day, you'll find the smaller streams bereft of steelheads.

This matter of water condition is all important to the steelheader who wants to be consistently successful. The type of year and the rainfall level actually dictates where and when the fishing should be done. There are four general rules that guide steelheading that should be kept in mind during the winter months: (1) On a dry year the angler should spend most of his time seeking out fish in the larger rivers. (2) During a wet season the odds on catching fish in the smaller rivers and creeks are better. (3) If it's a dry year fish closer to the mouth of the streams—where there is more water. (4) In a wet year fish closer to the headwaters of the streams.

This much is easily understood, but unfortunately weather during any given year does not conveniently divide itself into the clear cut definition of being either wet or dry. Instead, when rain arrives on the Pacific slope it will normally come in batches. Usually the series of rainstorms will ease off for a short period and then resume. On rare years the storms are so close together that they seem to be one gigantic downpour. These downpours can last for months on end, especially on the northern Oregon and the outer Washington coasts.

The best years are those in which the rains come early and heavy and then taper off and stop. When these conditions happen, steelheaders declare a vintage year because the steelheads come into the streams on the early freshets and then the ebbing flow stops them from further migration. The steelheaders can then pounce on the fish over a long stretch of time.

What the steelheader should consider is that he will always be forced to live with the conditions that nature provides. And right here I'd like to kill off a negative idea that has always inhibited the entire steelhead fishing fraternity. No matter how bad the weather seems to be, it is still possible to catch at least some steelheads. All that bad weather does is complicate the job of locating a run of fish, and rain is nothing more than a form of misery that every steelheader has got to learn to live with. I feel that instead of cussing the weather man the average angler would be much better off if he'd try to realize that without it there wouldn't be any steelheads for him to even try for.

Let's take a practical example of a single stream system and see what we can do about figuring out what an individual angler should do under winter conditions. I'll choose the Klamath River drainage because I am more familiar with this system than I am with those farther from my home. But the type of reasoning that I would use for fishing the Klamath drainage is exactly the same as I would use for fishing the streams in the Skeena-Kispiox drainage or any other throughout the range of the steelheads.

Let us suppose that we had decided to make a trip north from my home in the San Francisco Bay area. This is a journey of some 400 miles or about a nine-hour jaunt as westerners consider mileage. Let's also say that the trip is being made during the week after Christmas and before New Year's Day.

If you'll remember in the last chapter on summer and fall steelhead fishing I mentioned the important fact that even though the Klamath has always been famous for its August and September steelhead fishing in the portion of the river near Requa, at the mouth of the Klamath, we can take it for granted that the majority of the fish that entered the drainage have safely made it past the hordes of anglers who fish this part of the stream. And we can also safely assume that these early arriving fish have, by late December, spread themselves throughout the entire drainage. This means that we will look for fish in the middle and upper Klamath, the parent stream. It means that there are some fish in the Trinity River and also in any of the three major forks of the Trinity River drainage. And it means that the smaller Salmon River and Scott River also have some of the Klamath River migrants. When we say that we are going to fish the Klamath River we actually mean that we are able to choose from almost a thousand miles of stream, including the main stream, its major tributaries and even the smaller creeks if they are open to fishing at the time we are making the trip.

So here we are traveling north from San Francisco in an automobile (actually I use a pickup camper that makes me all but independent of sleeping and eating accommodations). During this nine-hour trip we have our radio tuned in and when the weather forecast comes over the air we find that a big storm has moved into the northern part of California where the Klamath River is located.

Weather reports as they come over the radio are not usually accurate enough for our purposes. In other words, a radio report would not indicate the extent of the rain that is falling on the Klamath watershed. The radio forecaster would probably only say that it was raining north of Eureka, a city on the coast of California. He could possibly say that it was raining lightly or heavily, but this condition of the weather could turn in either direction at any moment so it isn't very important to us as anglers. Let us assume that we have arrived about halfway, at the town of Redding, California, which is a centrally located stop where the highway system divides from east to west and north to south. Also, Redding is near enough to the drainage we are going to fish for us to stop and take stock of how the weather is going to affect our fishing effort.

If I arrived in Redding and knew that it was probably raining farther north, I'd take the time to make a couple of phone calls to selected spots on the key rivers of the drainage. I know whom to call because I have made cer-

tain to find these key locations on this drainage on pre-
vious trips. But anyone, even the beginner who has never
been on a steelhead fishing trip before, can get his hands
on a highway map and choose a couple of likely locations where phoning might pay off. Rural telephone
operators who service these isolated areas will, if told
what you want—to talk to someone, preferably a resort
owner or employee or a tackle shop operator in the area
who can give you the low-down on the weather—will be
able to connect you with someone who can simply look
out the window and say, "It's raining like hell." Or who
can tell you that the rain you heard reported on the radio
has passed or settled down to a drizzle. The whole operation of phoning from the halfway point of our journey
only takes a few minutes and it will cost far less than a
five dollar bill—about the cost of the gasoline you would
burn going these distances to look at the stream conditions for yourself.

Let's assume that our telephone contacts have given us
the information that a moderate rainfall is occurring
throughout the entire drainage of the Klamath. So we
know that we are in for a wet fishing trip and that the
water will probably be running bank full in most of
the streams. Here is where we make our final decisions
about where we are going to actually wet our lines on
this particular steelhead fishing trip. And it is at this
point that prior experience in fishing this particular
watershed is going to come into play.

I have fished through the Klamath drainage at least a
hundred times, so I know it like I know my own living
room. But anyone, even the rankest beginner, can provide himself with as many good maps as he can find
before making a trip into *any* drainage. These maps will
give him 90 per cent of the basic information that an

old-time steelheader has been able to acquire. I cannot stress too much how important these maps can be to the fisherman who wants to become a successful steelheader. Even after the angler has fished a drainage a hundred times he can still get ideas and information from maps. For the beginner they are absolutely essential if he doesn't want to end up stumbling around blindly in his search for a steelhead that will be willing to oblige him with a battle. I will assume that a beginner will take this map thing to heart and will be able to make some accurate estimates of what he is going to encounter when he actually gets to the soggy banks of his chosen steelhead stream.

To get back to that Klamath River fishing trip, we are going to commit ourselves to fishing a few locations. After a bit of debate with my memory, I would very probably turn off the north-south main highway U.S. 99 that intersects the Klamath River just above Yreka, California, and head due west out of Redding on Highway 299 that intersects the main fork of the Trinity River at Douglas City, California. A simple highway map could tell the beginner these things. But I would make this decision for a very specific reason.

The main fork of the Trinity River has a dam on it just above the hamlet of Lewiston. In fact, it has two dams on it, Lewiston Dam and Trinity Dam, located only a few miles apart. Both of these dams completely control the flow of water in the Trinity—just the same as any dam on any river completely dominates the flow of water on that river. This fact of a dam is available to anyone if they will merely look at any good highway map. But a fact that usually escapes most steelhead fishermen is that the stream below a dam for several miles will rarely be affected to any great extent by a current rainstorm. In effect, the dam holds back the flooding water provided by the current rainstorm and makes the stream conditions far more stable than they would have been if the dam were absent. So by merely choosing to fish the Trinity River in the area immediately below the Lewiston Dam I can be reasonably assured of more or less "normal" water conditions.

Of course, I have also taken into consideration several other elements when I made the decision to make my first fishing effort on the Trinity below the dam. I realized that this late in the season—Christmas week—the season has progressed far enough along so that a fair portion of the migrating steelheads that cut off from the main Klamath River had plenty of time to make the trip of some 150 miles up the Trinity to this specific area. As a matter of actual fact, prior experience has told me that this area of this particular stream will have at least a fair number of steelheads in it any time after the month of September. But anyway, let's assume that we fished this particular part of the Trinity for a day or so and that we got completely skunked. (This would be very unlikely under the conditions that we set up here for consideration of this particular steelheading problem. If we assume that we didn't catch any fish, we can go on to the solution of the problem of continuing our search for some winter steelheads in the Klamath drainage.) So it's time to get out our maps again and look for some other place to do our fishing.

By looking over the maps that any logical steelhead fisherman should have acquired before he ever makes any kind of steelhead fishing trip (especially during the winter months) we can see that there is another dam in the Klamath River drainage. This dam is the Iron Gate Dam located to the east of Highway U.S. 99 on the Klamath River. This dam controls the flow in the main Klamath River for several miles downstream, just the same as the Lewiston and Trinity Dams controlled the flow in the Trinity River. It would be the next logical spot for us to head for as long as we didn't manage to connect on the first try on the Trinity River.

Making the trip to Iron Gate Dam from the Trinity River entails going back east on Highway 299 to where it connects with the north-south U.S. 99 at the city of Redding. We'll assume that it has continued to rain all the time that we were fishing on the Trinity—a period of at least a couple of days.

At this point I would like to say that if it had quit raining during the period we were fishing the Trinity, and if the stream conditions had greatly improved, we should have made several phone calls to different locations in the whole drainage to find out whether the streams were clearing up quickly and how the local boys were doing with their fishing. It is very likely that if it had cleared up, we could have merely gone downstream on the Trinity River to meet any fish that were migrating due to the rainstorm that had been causing all of this trouble in the first place.

We make our next effort at catching some steelheads by fishing the area immediately below Iron Gate. And no matter how fierce the storm should get, we would still be able to fish the stream where it is almost at a normal level. If the storm should get so bad that it floods the Klamath River below Iron Gate we could merely return to the Trinity River and continue to fish it, because the Trinity is a much smaller stream and the pair of dams on it completely control the flow in this drainage no matter how bad the storm should get. I'd be willing to bet that if we fished hard, using these tactics at this time of year on this specific drainage we'd have one heck of a time not catching at least some steelheads.

All of this driving back and forth, figuring the effects

of dams on water flow, phoning around to check water conditions, and fishing long and hard might seem a complicated way of going about something that is supposed to be fun. But the beginner will have to take my word for it that this *is* an essential technique for consistent steelhead fishing success; as a matter of fact *these techniques are steelhead fishing.* The easiest part of steelhead fishing is the actual job of tempting a steelhead to strike your bait or lure once you've managed to locate a concentration of them. The steelhead has spent most of his life in the big world of salt water. He is not the least bit sophisticated about anglers, lures, or techniques of approach, as a stream-raised trout would be from living his entire life in water that is hard hit by hundreds and thousands of anglers. The steelhead is a visitor in the thousands of miles of streams draining into the Pacific Ocean, and he's got a mean streak in his makeup that was bred into him from generations of trying to make a living in a vicious, competitive salt water environment where he was just something else for other, larger fish to feed on if he didn't stay on his toes.

I do not claim, as some old timers do, that the steelhead is a piscatorial dumbbell; if he is fished for in clear, calm water he is as wary as any other trout. But this doesn't apply in rain swollen winter steelhead streams very often. So our main project in taking steelheads during any time of the year, and particularly during the winter months when there is more water to be fished, is to put ourselves where there are at least some steelheads available to fish over.

A few final notes on winter steelheading should fill in what will be a complete technique when taken with the other chapters. For instance, every steelhead stream has many side creeks, rivers, and brooks. Each of these smaller streams has an effect on the main or parent stream of the drainage. Whenever I notice a side stream I try to fish the area immediately adjacent to the mouth of these side streams with extra care. The reason for this is that most of these smaller creeks will get their quota of spawning steelheads sooner or later, depending on water conditions. And the steelheads that are going to move up into these streams will usually mill around the mouth of that creek until they consider conditions right for a trip up the smaller stream. This makes these stream mouths prime spots during the winter months in particular. Also, most of these side creeks will pour water into the main stream that is considerably clearer than the water in the parent stream, so the main stream is usually clearer just below the mouth of one of these smaller tributaries.

I will not go into the matter of what lure to use during the winter months. I guide my own winter fishing by only a few general principles. I rarely use bait myself in any form, although when the water is extremely discolored bait is all right because the steelheads are guided to it by scent even if they cannot see it in dirty water. What I do when I find myself stuck with fishing extremely dirty water is to merely change to lures that have more action.

I have caught steelheads in water so dirty that you'd think that running a plough through it would leave a furrow. I prefer rapidly whirling lures such as the Spin-N-Glow or a small spinner blade of any kind. The steelheads seem able to sense these rapidly moving blades in discolored water, and even if I were to use bait I would still attach some kind of whirling blade or lure immediately above the baited hook. As the water becomes clearer I usually will change to lures such as the Flatfish or

Guppy. If the water becomes clear enough so that I can see bottom in 18 in. I usually change over to heavily weighted flies. No matter what lure or fly I use during the winter months I try to fish it as close as possible to the bottom. This bottom flirting is the key to winter steelhead fishing success—once you've found the steelheads.

One other major point about winter steelhead fishing is worth noting before we go on: Rain water is normally warmer than the water in the stream during the winter months. It tends to pep the steelheads up a good deal and make them restless. The water may feel cold when it's falling on you personally, but it's not snow, and the stream water will nearly always be colder. And snow is rare in steelheading areas to any great extent.

Typical steelheads.

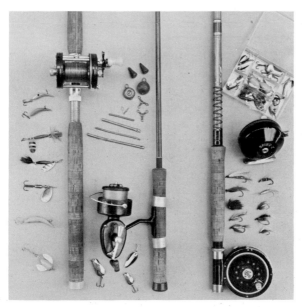

Rods, reels, and lures used for steelheads. Left is a modern level-
wind "meat rod" and center is a short spin outfit. Note in center
the selection of dropper weights for getting lures down to fish.
Right is a fly rod and fly rod spin reel for fishing uncertain
situations.

How distance casting champions use steelhead shooting heads.
This is Myron Gregory.

The typical "lineup" that the visiting angler should look for when he fishes a new stream. Local anglers usually know when there is a run of steelheads in a section of stream.

Combining a fly rod and a good fly rod spinning reel lets the fly fisherman work the water even when he can't get a backcast. Here, high brush didn't stop me from taking two nice summer run steelheads from a small coastal stream.

Fly casting in a typical "steelhead run." Note that the arm is not extended far to the rear. This is just a 70-ft. cast and full arm movement is not necessary.

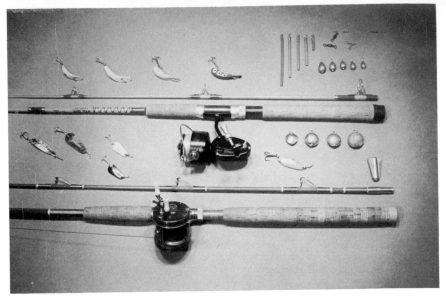

Modern drift fishing rigs. The spinning outfit is used with light weights and where moderate water is being fished. The "meat rod" is used for casting in heavy flowing water or for long distances.

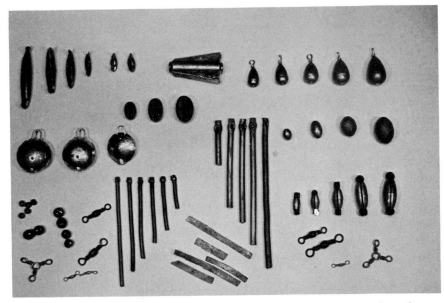

Just a few of the different types and sizes of weights that the steelhead fisherman should have on hand when he is actually on the stream fishing. They will allow him to fish all different types of water.

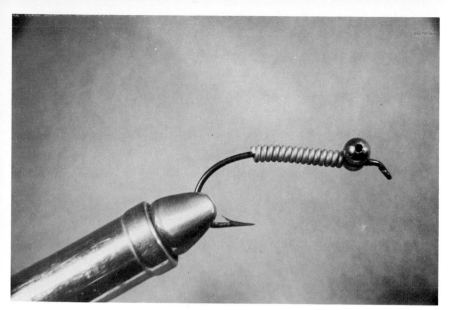

Two methods of adding weight to the hook: wrap fuse lead wire around the shank of the hook before the body material is tied on, and tie bead chain eyes on at front of fly.

Split shot should be added next to the knot and not some distance up the line. Pattern is one of the Boss type.

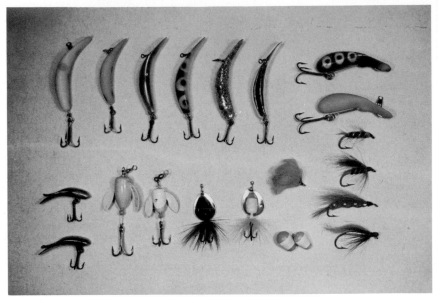

Floating or whirling types of lures used for steelhead fishing.
They represent the type of lure that needs weight added in order
to be fished. Thousands are on the market.

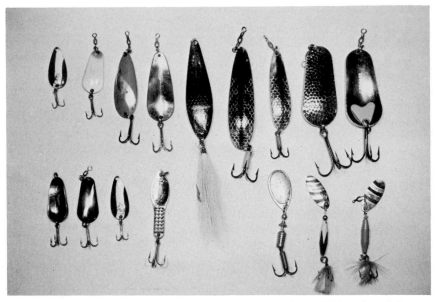

Metal lures that in most cases do not require additional weight
to be fished correctly.

A modern skin diving "wet suit" is ideal for wading in extremely cold water. Normally it is only necessary to use the bottom of the suit for complete warmth.

This sequence shows that even large winter steelheads can be handled with light tackle. The rod and reel used here are considered "ultra-light" for these winter fish. Note that the winter fish, being sluggish, are less likely to clear water on "jumps"; instead, they wallow.

This sequence illustrates the short, fishing type of double haul. Note that in no instance does the left (or pulling) arm go below waist level, where it would be submerged in water if angler were wading deep, as he would be in most cases.

Gather monofilament (preparatory to cast) between lips, with trailing loops of about 5 to 10 feet. These loops are allowed to trail down the front of the angler.

Short pull with *left* arm and backcast with right arm lifts and straightens line (30 ft.), shooting head and leader to rear.

Left arm *follows* backcast. Note how high rod is held. This gets line high and straight on backcast.

Right (casting) arm is cocked by dropping elbow. Left arm pulls
line before forward cast increases line speed. (It actually starts
screaming through the air at this point.)

Forward cast (right arm still kept *high*). Left arm completes fishing pull *horizontal* to water.

As fly line "shoots" forward, monofilament held between lips is released.

Release. As line passes rod tip, left hand releases. Excess monofilament "shooting line," in loose coils between lips up to this time, is released merely by opening the mouth.

The wading staff has more uses than aiding the angler with his wading. A three-fish limit of steelheads can weigh up to 50 or 60 lbs. This limit of 40 lbs. was strung on a favored sapling staff for easy return to camp.

Women can be just as thrilled with taking a huge steelhead as any man, once the fish have been located. My wife, Pat, caught this huge (20-lb.) steelhead in Thompson River, B. C., on light spinning tackle and 10-lb. test monofilament line.

10 Miscellaneous Steelhead Equipment

The subject of miscellaneous equipment that fits into steelhead fishing is a fertile field for conversation and debate among steelheaders. I do not know any two men who use exactly the same equipment. And I do not know of any two who will completely agree with each other on the subject. So all I can do here is point out and comment on the basic items that I feel the beginner should acquire and in which order these items should be purchased.

Any fisherman who has had much experience on the west coast steelhead streams will agree that the first two things to buy for the very first steelhead trip are a good rubberized parka and a stout pair of waders. These two basic garments will soon come to be as sacred and important as the pet rod and reel in the angler's gear.

Personally, I think that a parka should come down to about thigh length, at least. Some anglers even prefer to have the parka down past the knee—this is okay, even if a bit clumsy. The parka should be of good quality because it takes a tremendous beating even on a single trip and even the best are in pretty sorry shape after an entire season. The hood on the parka should be ample. A small hood will let a driving rain seep around the face and before lunch the angler will be wet to the stomach. I also always put a medium-sized bath towel around my shoulders when I'm fishing on a really rainy day. The towel stays in place if it's draped over the shoulders underneath the parka even if you have to do a lot of climbing, and it soaks up a lot of the rain that seeps inside of any parka hood. Also, I use heavy rubber bands wrapped around the outside of the parka sleeves so these openings are completely sealed. If you don't use these rubber bands water from your hands will dribble up your sleeves at least as far as your elbow even on a mildly rainy day because your hands in fishing are nearly always pointing upward.

I like waders that come up to armpit height, although most of the waders I see other anglers using are chest high models. I think that the angler buying his first pair of waders should invest in common boot foot waders. There are several types of waders found in steelhead country and many anglers swear by insulated boot foot waders. However, I haven't found that the insulation actually makes too much difference after a few hours of wading. And thermal boot waders are a misery if you have to walk any distance. I also like a pair of stocking foot waders that have wading shoes over them. These are the most logical items to have if you are going to do much climbing or distance walking. However, they are pretty cold affairs as a general rule. I haven't tried out the waders that go over the tops of a pair of shoes, but some of my buddies who do a lot of serious wading tell me that though they are expensive to use, they are the warmest of all the different types of waders. Still, the common boot foot seems like the logical initial purchase.

Hip boots are handy items to have on any steelhead fishing trip. They are okay for bank fishing and they are handy around camp when it's raining. When worn with a good parka the angler is just about water proof until he tries some serious wading. Also, many places where steelheading is good are best fished from the bank.

It's odd that I rarely see other steelhead fishermen who carry a common umbrella with them when they go steelheading. I do not mean that I expect them to take it along when they are trying to fish—except when they are plunking. But nothing can beat a rainstorm around camp like an umbrella. It is the perfect item to use to pop down to the stream to wash your face or get some water from a tap. If the angler is taking any pictures the umbrella is perfect for protecting the camera. For a few dollars a cheap umbrella is worth taking along.

The subject of thermal underwear soon becomes a thing dear to the hearts of all steelheaders who fish during the winter months. I fished for years without thermal underwear, but I was much younger then, and if I couldn't have the comfort provided by a good selection of thermals today, I know I would do far less steelhead fishing during the winter months.

The warmest type of thermal underwear I've used are the quilted jobs. You end up looking like a Chinese communist soldier, but the warmth they provide far override the effects on your beauty from these bulky garments. When you wade just one hour in near icy water, you'll come to love these quilted long johns.

The next type of underwear to consider is the double

type that has cotton on the inside and a layer of wool on the outside. These are nice to have around on any cool morning. I normally have at least two pairs of underwear. A good choice would be one pair of double folds and a pair of quilted thermals. This way you can get out of the quilted ones in the evening and hang them up to dry while you put the double folds on for evening warmth and maybe to sleep in.

I have a pair of underwear that look like nothing more than a fishing net cut to fit the human body. These netted affairs are surprisingly warm and just about right for beating the cold on a fall morning. Then when the sun comes up and the canyons start to sizzle, these nets let the perspiration out. Also, there is absolutely nothing wrong with the old fashioned long johns if they are 100 per cent pure wool. And good long johns, if they are treated right and washed often, will last nearly a lifetime.

The past few years I've been experimenting with using skin diving suits for steelhead fishing when the temperature really gets low as it does in the northern part of the range. These bottoms of a skin diving wet suit are certainly warm and I recommend them to anyone who suffers a great deal from severe cold. They are quite a bit of trouble to get in and out of, but they are the best thing I've ever seen to beat the cold. You merely wear them and nothing else on the bottom half of your body. They're reasonably priced too, and the nylon models are tough enough to take a lot of use.

Most anglers will get very cold feet when they are fishing for steelheads. I've tried just about everything to get around cold feet but nothing really seems to work. The most practical way to go about keeping your feet warm is to wear at least two pair of medium weight all wool stockings and change them when you stop for lunch each day. But I have developed an idea that I feel has merit. If your feet really get too cold, it is very probable that you aren't moving around enough. Walking always seems to warm up my own feet, and I rarely am bothered by cold feet if I am moving around enough trying to locate fish. I've tried the quilted model stockings but don't use them anymore because they soon mat down and are less effective than the common wool stockings. I've tried stockings that were warmed chemically and with batteries, but I've given them up as impractical. The cure for cold feet is movement!

I would say that any steelhead angler who wants to become serious about the game should get hold of a boat or raft of some sort just as soon as he can afford one. However, owning a boat could be said to be a vital element of just about any kind of fishing because it gets you where the fish are. Personally, I always prefer to fish from my two feet for any fish but particularly for steelheads. But I've lost track of the number of times that I've had to use a boat to get to the fish. This is particularly true if you decide to fish the lower stretches of most rivers where you are dealing with tidal areas.

My own choice for a boat is a 12 ft. aluminum craft. This boat has 22 in. depth and is 60 in. in the beam. It is small enough to be wrestled into tight spots, yet it is big enough to take a beating from a big river or a windy bay. I wouldn't be caught on any fishing trip without it. I run it with a 10 hp motor that pushes it along fast enough to get me over long distances quickly. But I do think that any kind of boat is preferable to no boat at all. Even a cheap rubber raft is extremely handy to have along. If nothing else, you can row to the other side of a river and get away from most of the crowds in many cases.

I have tried many different types of gloves to try to keep my hands warm when steelhead fishing. The types I've tried went all the way from rubber gloves like the ones surgeons use or that the wife uses to do dishes to bulky gloves that have a compartment for a hand warmer. None of them ever satisfied me, so I've learned to live with cold hands and fingers when I go steelheading. The best gloves I ever owned were wool inside and composition plastic on the outside. They didn't have fingers in them, so I suppose you could call them mittens. I carry these mittens with me, especially when I'm fishing from a boat, but they actually rarely get used because I find it so difficult to fish with anything on my hands. So the question of proper hand warmers is left in a limbo from which I doubt that it will ever emerge.

I never use a gaff on a steelhead. I'd much rather lose a fish than jab a thing like a gaff into him. When I'm fishing from a boat I like to have a net about 24 in. across with a handle about 2½ ft. to 3 ft. in length. I've never had any trouble handling even 20 lb. fish with this net, and it is a regular part of my steelhead fishing gear but only when I'm fishing from a boat. I use neither gaff nor net when I am wading or bank fishing. I have lost a few fish because of this, but I feel that anything as large as a net would be too much trouble to fight through the brush at streamside or to wade with. The fish that I have lost because of not having a net are rare. It's part of good steelheading technique to consistently keep an eye on the situation and make reasonably certain that you'll have a place to land a fish if you should happen to hook one. It will become a habit after you lose a couple of big ones, believe me.

I see many steelhead fishermen toting tackle boxes and

creels on the stream. I never use either. A tackle box is out of the question when you are moving constantly as I do. But if the angler is a plunker he might just as well bring a tackle box along for convenience sake. I use a gas mask container that I've owned for about 15 years. The gas mask container costs less than a dollar and the feature I like about it is that it has an additional strap that goes around the waist and takes the weight off the neck. They are extremely rugged bags and you can load them down with all the gear you'll ever be likely to need —probably a lot of junk, too, if you're like me when it comes to trying new lures or rigs. I think that a good creel would be nearly as good, but I would want it to be plastic or some tough material. I wouldn't want to fight a reed creel through miles of brush. They are much too bulky. As far as using a creel to hold the fish, it would be impossible. You couldn't get a limit of steelheads into even the largest creel. The fish are too big.

I see a lot of anglers using wading staffs of either wood or metal. I've tried many and have given them up. Again, they get in the way when I move around. However, I usually have one along on the trip. Some rivers are so treacherous that it would be all but suicidal to try wading without one. But I try to avoid them. After all, I can always carry a short length of light clothesline and cut a wading staff on the spot. In many places, where I repeatedly cross a river and return often, I even take the time to stash the wading staff I've cut in a convenient place so that I can use it the next time I return. This way I've always got one handy when I need it. In fact, some of the staffs that I use on rivers that I fish a lot are several seasons old. One I can think of on the upper Klamath—a monstrous stream to wade—is at least five seasons old. They get to be like old friends, and I sort of like the idea of coming back for them on succeeding years.

I use a fishing vest especially when I am fly fishing. The model I use has a lot of extra pockets into which I can stuff endless gear. I have never found anything more practical than a good commercially made fishing vest of better quality. I've tried to design them but something is always wrong with the ones I've had my wife sew up for me. I've finally settled for good commercial models. They seem outrageously expensive for what they give you, but they are good once you get over the shock of their initial price. The only thing I wish is that the zippers in the ones I've used were of better quality. If they are going to go wrong it's in the zipper department where they go astray.

I always wear dark glasses when I fish during all but the rainiest weather. I have several pair of polarized lenses that I use for two reasons. Polarized glasses allow you to see down into the water almost 20 per cent better than the naked eye. I've spotted many underwater boulders and obstructions with them that I would have missed had I not used them. And when I fly fish I always use polaroids because they protect my eyes from that whizzing fly. If the wind whips the fly in the direction of your head there is every chance that it could take your eye with it. It's a small item of expense, and I think anyone foolish who doesn't take this easy precaution, even if they don't think that polarized lenses are worth the trouble.

I also always wear a hat when I fish. I have several different kinds. When I am wearing a parka I use a plastic or leather hat with a visor. This helps to keep the rain from pelting my face, and visors are good eye shades if the sun is up. As a secondary reason, they keep your ears warm if they are fitted with a band that pulls down, not to mention that they keep your head warm. I use a hat with a brim when the sun shines, because I blister from the sun if I don't.

There are many aids that waders use to help them do a better job of moving around in the water. I have had my best results with felt soled wading aids that fit right over the foot of the wader boot. There are many different materials used for these attachments like aluminum, steel, and even lengths of chain. The purpose of these is usually to bite down through the slime that coats underwater rocks and gravel and to be able to get a grip so that the wader won't be swept off his feet. The aluminum attachments have proved best for me with metal aids and the chain next best. I have seen some anglers who had their wader shoes fitted with an additional sole into which they could screw golf or football cleats. These are swell if you find yourself wading on clay, but they act like an ice skate if you step on a slick, flat rock. I would suggest that the beginner stick with a pair of boot foot waders and then merely get the felt soled aids that fit over the boots. Then if the beginner finds that some other form of attachment is necessary for a specific river he happens to be fishing he can usually find them in a local tackle shop. In short, let experience guide in the selection of these items. One thing though, always take the aid off when you get out of the water and start heading back to camp. These long walks over dry ground will wear them out faster than anything.

Oddly enough, one of the most important items a steelhead fisherman should carry when he goes out for a day of fishing is an extra pair of shoes that are light and compact. I use a pair of low tennis shoes. I carry the waders bundled up if I have to do any serious walking to get to streamside. Then when I'm actually on the stream I put on the waders and merely slip the shoes into the pocket in the front of the waders. When I'm ready to make the long walk back to camp I take the waders off and put the tennis shoes back on. You'd be surprised how much easier walking is especially if you're carrying a couple of large fish at the same time. Naturally, if the distances you are covering are not considerable there is no sense in taking along this extra pair of light shoes. Extra stockings are always handy and take up a small amount of space.

I haven't mentioned the automobile as a piece of miscellaneous equipment that the steelheader should have on any trip. I've harped enough in other chapters about the necessity for moving around perpetually until you locate the fish. I will say though, that a pickup camper is a handy item to have if you can spare the money to get a good rig together. My own rig with the aluminum boat on the top of it has paid for itself many times over in all of my outdoor activities.

11 Fly Casting for Steelheads

The technique of "long line" fly casting is by no means an easy thing to learn. It looks very simple when you see it done, and it is actually easy to do once you have mastered the basic steps.

In Chapter 3, I outlined the idea that the caster is merely casting weight when he uses any type of rod, including a fly rod. But long line fly casting is more than merely rigging a fly line a different way. It is an entirely different process than the common fly casting technique used by trout or black bass fishermen. The object in long line casting is distance, so the equipment is put together for this reason more so than for any other. When a shooting head is cast to a hundred feet or more just about every semblance of delicacy disappears. In many cases, the whole 30 ft. length of the shooting head will land on the water in a massive, ungainly blob.

Most of us try to avoid this lack of delicacy, but there

really isn't much that can be done about this factor of the technique. In any case the fly lines used for steelhead fishing are heavy and even the shortest cast will land on the water with a lot of commotion. It's probably a good thing that the average steelhead holds in swift water and that they are not too spooky as a breed. If they were as wary as a stream raised trout far less would ever be hooked and landed.

Starting with the business end, the leader, I'll try to outline the techniques involved in long lining. The leaders used for steelhead fishing are usually pretty coarse when compared to trout leaders. The general consensus among most steelheaders is that an 8 ft. or 9 ft. level leader is all that is needed for most steelhead fishing. Some steelhead fly fishermen insist that the leader tippet should not exceed 6 lb. test for summer fishing—due to the clarity of the water. I don't go along completely with either of these notions.

First of all, it is a simple matter to make up a tapered leader by just starting out with a heavy piece of monofilament that measures about the same diameter as the end of the fly line. Then taper the leader in steps until you get down to the desired tippet strength. And I feel that a level leader can never turn a fly over as well as a properly tapered model. Because it is so easy to tie up a good tapered leader, this is how I rig my own fly fishing gear. I like a leader about 9 ft. in length because it is a convenient length, but if it is a bit longer or shorter, it doesn't bother my fishing a bit.

I started out using 4 lb. and 6 lb. tippets for my own steelhead fishing because all the old duffers who were around at that time told me this was best. But when you use a leader of even 6 lb. test material you will lose an amazing number of steelheads. In fact, it is extremely difficult to avoid this because when a steelhead is hooked on a sinking line there is normally some slack in the line that you've already started to retrieve. The steelhead feels the bite of the barb and takes off like a rocket. When he runs to the point where all of the slack is gone out of the line he is going pretty fast and when the moving line tries to start the heavy reel spool revolving it does so with a tremendous amount of energy. The leader usually will break at this point. Of course, if you can get past this point and start playing the fish from the reel—as all steelheads should be played—6 lb. test leader and tippet material is usually enough. So, at the present time the smallest tippets I normally use, even for summer fishing, test 8 lbs. or more. I have no doubt that I would hook more fish in clear water with smaller tippets, but what's the sense of hooking the fish and then not being able to land a good percentage of them?

Most shooting heads that match the action of a given rod should do so somewhere near the 30 ft. length that the ready-made commercial lines come in. A foot or so one way or the other in length doesn't matter very much, but if the homemade shooting head goes much past 33 ft. in length it starts to become awkward to manipulate on the average stream. If much shorter than 28 ft., the tempo of casting is speeded up to an uncomfortable degree.

The same thing is true when the angler goes about the process of weighing up a line for a shooting head. A matter of ten grains one way or the other isn't very important, although there are plenty of anglers who insist that they can feel or tell the difference in lines that are a few grains this way or that. Personally, I just let this kind of guy quibble and go about my own fishing.

This matter of weighing up and making a shooting

head from a double taper line seems to confuse many people. The process is very simple, though. You merely choose a commercial line that has the correct weight classification for the rod that you are going to use it on. And even deciding what the correct weight is is a simple process if the rod is an old favorite from many past seasons.

I'll take it for granted that a pet rod has been functioning okay in the past with the line that is on it. If you want to determine what weight line it currently has on it, you just rig it up and take it out on the front lawn or sidewalk. You work out a length of line that seems comfortable by repeatedly false casting. When the line weight is putting a fair strain on the rod so that you can feel it loading up on each forward and backward cast, let the line fall to the ground. Do not strip off any more line from the spool; instead, mark and coil up the line that is *past the tip of the rod.* To keep it in this coil, just wrap a common pipe cleaner around it. Then take the whole works down to the corner drugstore and ask the man to weigh the coiled section *only* and to tell you how many grains of line weight you have in that section. Most druggists will be glad to do this.

Of course, if you are a hunter and own a reloading scale used for powder measurements, you can use this scale instead of having a druggist do the job. But what you want to know is how many grains of line weight is just right for you, your technique, and that particular rod. The next step is to go to a good tackle shop and buy a double taper line that weighs the same amount. You can double check this by using the table in Chapter 3. Or you can buy a shooting head already made up and ready to go.

I like to use the shooting heads that are already made

up, but if they aren't available in the weight I want I will make up my own. To make a homemade shooting head you just cut the first 30 ft. of line off the double taper. Be sure to check that the particular line that you have bought doesn't have a long length of level line at the very tip. If it does have this level line on the end you have to cut it off because the line will never cast well, and it will not weigh the stated amount for the first 30 ft.

The next step is to put a 2 in. section of both ends of the line into a bottle of fingernail polish remover. Any commercial solvent that will cut the finish off the line is alright, but fingernail polish remover is usually the most convenient thing to use. After both ends of the line have soaked for about five minutes you can scrape the coating off them with your thumbnail. This leaves only the core of the line, actually a braided line.

The next step is to fray the ends of the bared, braided line until all of the strands are separated for about a half inch. Then you bend the line back onto itself and wrap it smoothly until it forms a loop in each end of the line. The threads of the winding material are then coated with fly head cement, spar varnish or any other material, such as fingernail polish or plastic paint. The function of coating is merely done to anchor the winding threads and keep them from coming loose due to rubbing against the guides of the rod. A fairly thick coating is best.

There is a shorter process for connecting either the butt end of the leader to a modern nylon or dacron fly line or shooting head. It is called tying a nail knot. The knot (see the illustration) is merely a matter of tying the end of the monofilament over itself, much as you would if you were tying on the thread over a metal guide or ferrule. The illustrations are self-explanatory. But it should be mentioned that these knots have to be tied with care and that they should be tested vigorously before you go on a trip. If a heavy fish hits and these knots slip, the entire trip could well be ruined because the angler forgot to take along an extra shooting head and is unable to locate the right head in the area where he is fishing. These nail knots will bite down into a synthetic coated line and hold well, but they should not be used if the angler is using silk line. Silk does have this collapsing covering feature that holds the monofilament and the fly line securely.

The final process is to load the reel and tie on the leader. First, fill the reel about half way with common braided fishing line testing about 20 lb. or 25 lb. Then tie on about 100 ft. of monofilament. Do not use more than about 100 ft. because it may destroy the reel as I pointed out in Chapter 3. Now tie the rear end of the shooting head through the loop you've formed to the 20 lb. test monofilament with a simple jam knot using about four to six turns. Then tie the butt section of the leader through the loop in the tip end of the shooting head. Both of these loops, with a simple jam knot, will easily slide through the guides of any rod.

Now you are ready to do some long line casting. The simplest way to do it is to merely work the shooting head out of the guides by false casting until the head is about 3 ft. past the tip top. Once you've reached this point you make one more false cast and let the line go. The fly line will "shoot" out, trailing the monofilament line. Within a few minutes any angler who has ever used a fly rod at all will automatically add 20 ft. or more to the longest cast he's ever managed to make in his life using double taper lines. The same goes for any angler who has used a weight forward or torpedo taper line.

I am not going to go into a long or detailed description of "double hauling" or points of release here, because I have never seen anything practical in either writing or in illustrations that ever did me any good from among the hundreds of books I've read. Instead I suggest that the beginner, and even the old timer who is new at the game of long lining, should try something new.

If there is a good casting club nearby I heartily suggest that the reader go there and see if there are any distance fly casters as members. These fellows can shorten the time necessary for anyone trying to learn long lining. And they can straighten out any mistakes made much quicker than the angler can by himself. But if there isn't a club handy the cause is still not hopeless if the angler is willing to spend some time learning by himself.

The critical place in fly casting is the backcast. There is only one way you can find out what the backcast is doing and that is to turn your head around and look at it. Every tournament distance caster I've ever seen who amounted to anything turned his head around to see what that backcast was doing. So if it's good enough for them, it's good enough for me.

One idea that has worked for me when I am attempting to show a beginner how to cast is based on a movie camera. I use a cheap 8 mm. camera; any film is good enough. It is almost impossible to tell a beginner exactly what he is doing wrong, because most beginners make several mistakes at the same time. But if I just shoot a 100 ft. of film, have it developed, and then point out these errors one by one, the beginner can then judge for himself by seeing himself in action on film. And he can run the film as many times as he needs to until he is casting correctly.

Another good idea is to take a roll or two of movie

film of some good long liners whenever you get a chance to see them in action. This can even be done out on the stream if the beginner doesn't happen to know a good caster personally. In this way the beginner can then have something to judge himself against; and by repeatedly running both rolls of film and working on his own technique he will eventually become a competent caster. I feel that this is the best method for the person who is determined to learn this phase of steelheading. It's a bit complicated, to be sure, but I know of no other way to go about the job of learning the techniques required.

Now, once the angler learns the heady art of throwing a fly line for long distances he usually needs to be cautioned about its uses and abuses. Most long liners have to go through a stage of fly casting wherein they develop a sort of mania for distance. I went through this myself, so I can speak from experience. But now I will never make a cast any longer than is absolutely necessary to cover the water I am fishing. It took me a long time to learn the simple, logical fact that most long liners never learn. The fact is: There are just as many steelheads on this side of the river as there are over there on the other side! And the water should be fished as methodically as you would with any other type of tackle. This methodical coverage should be followed until you learn where the fish are laying in each new pool. Then you might try just fishing the stretches that have proved successful from past experience.

Fly fishing success in steelhead fishing usually depends on two things: how well you cover all of the available water, and how deep you fish.

At the present time dacron is the fastest sinking material from which fly lines are made. This is the line material that I suggest for the first fly line the beginner buys. Nylon sinks less rapidly and purchasing one of these can wait. The older silk lines have a sinking weight somewhere between that of nylon and dacron. I have a few silk shooting heads but I rarely ever use them.

I usually have at least two lines with me on the stream when I am fishing. I keep a spare coiled in my pocket. If you coil and wrap these spare lines with a pipe cleaner they do not get tangled in your pocket. It is a simple matter to change lines when you are using shooting heads, and many times I've lost shooting heads when a very big fish took the route over the rapids and I couldn't follow. It's cheap insurance because a single fishing trip usually costs more than the cost of an extra line. Remember, if you make up your own shooting heads you get two of them out of each double taper you chop up.

To round off this chapter I'll make a few comments on techniques and angling traditions that I've run across in my years on the steelhead streams. If an angler says that he can get more distance out of a weight forward or torpedo taper line than he can out of a shooting head I would never argue with him. But the beginner who doesn't have any built in prejudices can take my word for it that the fellow is kidding himself. It is a physical impossibility for him to get more distance with these old fashioned lines. The monofilament shooting line that is tied on at the butt of the shooting head is about as small and as slick surfaced as any product now on the market, so it affects the running of the line through the guides less than any other material. But the important thing to me as a fisherman is that this monofilament lets me fish much deeper, because it also offers less resistance to the flow of water past it as the shooting head sinks. These things can add up to those few critical inches of extra depth that can mean the difference between success and failure.

I have given short shrift to the subject of double hauling (or pulling the line with the hand not holding the fishing rod) mainly because describing, or even teaching beginners the technique, has me completely baffled. It would take several chapters the length of this one to point out all the possible points where a beginner might make mistakes. And then I doubt that anything would be accomplished. I'll let the subject go with a statement to the effect that learning to double haul the line in steelhead fishing is extremely helpful. It is the measure of how far you will ever be able to throw the line in the long run. By all means learn the technique as soon as possible. One cautioning note on double hauling is worth noting. If a tournament caster teaches you the technique you will have to vary it on the stream. A tournament caster makes a "full double haul." This means that he pulls on the front and back cast clear down to his knees —even bending to get a longer pull. While this is alright on the tournament pools, you would end up with your arm buried to the elbow in the water if you were to try a full haul while deep wading. I always try to double haul parallel with the surface of the ground or water. This way I get about three-fourths of the effects of a full haul. The illustrations show this in action. Being right handed I end up with my left hand stretched out from my left side away from the body.

When I fish with a fly I try to keep my false casting to an absolute minimum. One of the truest sayings is that you can never catch a fish while the line is in the air. And because I am a crank about such things I never pull the rear end of the shooting head into the guides. Instead, I retrieve the line until the butt of the shooting head is flush with the tip top of the rod. Then I roll cast once or twice to get the line to the surface. As the roll cast completes its turn over I catch it by backcasting just as the fly turns over in the air. I make one or two false casts changing direction if necessary and dropping the necessary two or three feet of monofilament past the tip top. Then I let the cast go just as soon as possible. In this way, by not bringing the fly line into the guides, I feel that I get much more actual fishing done than an angler who spends a lot of time making these useless false casts merely getting the shooting head out of the guides. In a full day of steelhead fishing perhaps a thousand casts are made and this feature of technique can make a great deal of difference as far as success is concerned.

Every year I see anglers fishing greased line techniques and trying to take steelheads with dry flies and with flies fished near the surface. Only a few times have I seen situations where these techniques have paid off. But they are so rare that I would not recommend that anyone should spend very much time fooling around with them unless the angler knew something very special. I've taken a few steelhead by each of these methods, but I can count on the fingers of one hand the number of times I've seen these ocean going species rise to a fly that is floating on the surface. This makes sense to me. How much food did the fish ever see floating on the surface during the major portion of their lives when they were deep in salt water?

As a parting shot for this chapter, let me suggest that any extra time spent on techniques in fly fishing be used correcting the backcast. Try to train yourself to keep the backcast as high as humanly possible. Remember, the higher you can keep that backcast the better you will cast. More important from a practical steelhead fishing point of view, you can cast over the top of streamside brush if that backcast is high. This matter of beating the brush situation with a high backcast has put many a steelhead on my stringer!

12 Special Steelhead Fishing Methods

Every day a "practical" steelhead fisherman is stuck with the job of choosing exactly which type of equipment he will use for that day's fishing. (By practical, I mean the type of angler who does not consider himself either a fly fisherman or a spin fisherman, or some other kind of one-method fisherman.) I'd like to suggest a special type of rig that I've used for many years in the majority of cases when this matter of choice has some latitude. By having a choice I'm referring to the type of stream, and the type of stream conditions where the use of a single method is not dictated in advance.

In each and every case I will choose a fly rod as my kind of fishing equipment, if I've got a choice. But I long ago gave up the idea of trying to take steelheads with *only* a fly rod outfit. And because I like to fish logically and because I like to catch fish, I found that I was fishing more and more with spinning gear. This bothered me to such an extent that I tried to find some method of being able to have the mobility of spin fishing and the aesthetic joys of fly fishing. The reason for this is because the majority of steelhead streams in the Pacific slope drainage only have a small portion of them in which fly fishing is logical. I'd say that at most, 10 per cent of the available water is ideal for fly fishing. This is due to the trouble a fly fisherman has getting a backcast. And the net result is that the fly fisherman either has to pass up 90 per cent of the available water (which is ridiculous) or choose other methods of fishing each day.

At first I tried just carrying two rods: a fly rod broken down and stuffed into the top rear of my waders, and a spinning rod carried set up and ready to go. But this proved unfeasible in the long run. It seemed as though I was always running back and forth retrieving my spinning rod or my fly rod when I was done fishing a stretch of water with one type of gear or the other. So, I found a method to combine both types of equipment and still benefit from both of them.

I now carry a fly rod spinning reel in the pocket of my fly fishing vest and a selection of lures meant for steelhead spin fishing. These fly rod spinning reels are pretty hard to find nowadays, but they were very popular when spin fishing first came to the U.S. from Europe right after World War II. I prefer these fly rod models, but any enclosed spool spin or spin casting reel will do a fair job of making a basic fly fishing outfit much more practical than if you merely were to use it as a fly outfit alone.

It is very little bother to either change from one reel to the other or to carry the necessary gear with you while on the stream.

When I come to a stretch of stream that can be fished logically with a fly rod I have the rig set up for fly fishing.

When I come to a stretch where fishing a fly is difficult or impossible to fish with a fly rod, I merely reach into my pocket, replace the fly reel with the fly rod spin reel and continue to fish through that stretch until I come to another area where fishing a fly makes sense.

Naturally, the fly rod spin fishing reel is not as practical on an all around spin fishing basis as the regular open faced spinning reel, but it is adequate for most situations. And I have the added benefit of being able to offer virtually all the available fish a variety of lures and baits. I feel that these spin casting reels are definitely a good investment for the angler who is by choice a fly fisherman, but who still wants to do a more or less logical and practical job of covering all the available water.

As a general rule, steelhead streams are strong flowing waters. But there are several streams in each major area that have big, still pools that are usually pretty deep. The tidal stretches of even the largest steelhead streams have areas where the water is virtually at a stand still. And any stream, no matter how mean it is, has some deep still stretches. I'd say that the majority of the fishing pressure on most streams, especially the local angling talent, is wasted on these basically poor steelhead fishing pools.

The steelhead, by nature, is a restless creature. He is nervous in flowing, fresh water, because he has spent most of his life in limitless stretches of salt water. He likes the comfort and security of the deeper riffles where he is somewhat protected from the strangeness of this new environment. When a steelhead holes up in deep, still water he is usually tired from the rigors of his journey and not in a feeding or fighting mood. This is the reason that deep, still pools are poor areas to catch steelheads. But there is one method that I've found that at least gives the pool angler a chance. I call it "crawling for steelheads."

Crawling has a long history in the steelheading world. Before World War II, there were only two types of gear available to steelhead fishermen. Fly fishing was one method and baitcasting was the other. But when the fly fisherman found himself beaten by streamside brush or by still water, he would take the fly reel off the rod and replace it with a cheap fly reel loaded with very light line. Then he'd "strip cast." Strip casting is nothing more than pulling off a convenient quantity of the light line, letting it fall to the ground or the bottom of the boat, hooking a baited hook or lure to the far end, and lobbing the whole clumsy business out into the water.

As you can imagine, strip casting was a specialized thing although some anglers that I've known became surprisingly adept at the game. The big drawback to strip casting is that that glob of line that lays coiled at your feet is unreasonably difficult to keep from tangling. It gets into everything and hooks every conceivable protrusion. With the coming of spinning gear, even the stoutest supporter of strip casting converted over to the more convenient spin fishing equipment. The unfortunate part of the conversion is that spinning gear is so convenient and quick to use that the fine art of moving a lure or a bait along the bottom slowly was lost in the shuffle.

In a deep, clear, still piece of water any lure or bait that moves along very fast will scare the scales off resting steelheads. The entire trick to making them strike under these circumstances is to move the bait or lure right on the bottom at an excruciatingly slow pace. You simply cannot go too slowly, and yet you are defeating your purpose of covering the water if you merely cast the bait or lure out and let it lay on the bottom. So for my own crawling I use light spinning gear and fish as slowly as my temperament will let me.

The best thing to use for crawling is fresh bait. A gob of fresh roe is probably tops, but a fat night crawler is good, as is a fresh shrimp impaled on the hook and with a toothpick driven up through its body to keep the shrimp straightened out in a natural position. The reason that bait is best is that a lot of terminal tackle is lost because crawling along the bottom repeatedly will certainly detect any form of snag or obstruction in a pool. Each time I find a snag I lose another hook and bait, but it's a lot cheaper to lose a one cent hook than it is to lose a one dollar lure every time I locate a snag.

For my own crawling I like to use a boat if it is at all feasible. The reason for a boat is twofold: First, it gives me a measure of mobility so that I can place the boat in the exact position that I want to cover the place where I think the fish are holding. Next, I can use extremely light tackle and when the hooked steelhead takes off I merely flip the anchor rope—which has a float on it—and follow the fish wherever he leads.

The very best crawling gear consists of 4 lb. or 6 lb. test monofilament. With this light line I can cast a plain baited hook a good distance. The weight of the hook alone is usually enough to take the whole works to the bottom in still water. A few split shot are all that is ever necessary to take the bait down. I even know a couple of purists at crawling who use shotgun pellets that they split with a sharp blade and bite onto the line to get exactly the right amount of weight on the end of the line for critical crawling. And if you need any more weight than a few split shot you are fishing in water that is better for drift fishing rather than for this delicate business of working dead water.

What the technique of crawling amounts to is rowing up cautiously to a spot, easing the anchor over the side as gently as possible, baiting up with as delicate a terminal rig as possible, and then repeatedly casting upstream and walking the bait downstream into the holding area of the pool. When you manage to hook a steelhead of fair size under these conditions, I will guarantee that you will be busier than a cat trying to cover up three mouse holes with two paws. This is the way I like my own fishing because the light gear gives the fish all the odds.

Another method that is special because you don't run across the situations to suit it too often, I call "waking for steelheads." I've found that steelheads that run during the early fall months when the water is fairly warm in most streams will react with startling action if you strip a fly in as fast as possible. Why they do this, I don't know. But I would suspect that these fish, fresh in from the ocean, have been used to chasing some form of bait that moves fast, just under the surface of the water.

Anyway, the technique is to use a dry fly line. I use a floating shooting head, but a double taper is all right for this fishing. I grease the line, but rub the leader with sand to make sure that it sinks. The flies I use for this kind of fishing are rather small for general steelhead fishing. The best sizes are tied on No. 8 and No. 10 hooks. A common bucktail pattern has always been best for me, though I suppose any other might be just as effective. Most of my favorite patterns for waking are dark flies, but I've had some luck with a few bright patterns. All of these flies are tied in the common wet fly manner using limp hackles to promote sinking.

You rig up with a greased fly line, a sinking leader tapered to about 6 lb. test monofilament, and then tie on a fly that is fairly small. Then start casting; but as soon as the fly hits the water, start stripping it back in as fast as it can be brought into the tip of the rod. Also, never stop shuffling your feet as you move continually along the stretch of river or tidal pool that you are fishing. What you are trying to do is bring that sinking pattern back in so fast that it virtually leaves a wake, complete with a trailing "Vee" in the water.

The reason to keep continually moving along is that the line smacking down on the water, and the fly darting along just below the surface of the water have done either one of two things. The fish has either been attracted by the commotion and struck the darting fly out of reflex action or you've scared the fins off him and he's high-tailing it out of the area.

I've had many good days of fishing with this waking technique, especially fishing on those days when you can see fish splashing around but they don't seem to want anything that you throw at them. The technique has never worked for me during the winter months when the water is cold. It has been best when the water was very clear, the sky overcast, and the water fairly warm. But it is explosive fishing. I've seen fish frantically chasing the fly as if they were demented. They splash like a surface feeding black bass, and they will follow the fly, slashing at it in a frenzy even though they miss it continually. When the situation is right, this kind of fishing is even better than dry fly fishing. It is much like the common riffling hitch fishing that some fly anglers use to tempt Atlantic salmons. The only big drawback is that it is extremely tiring on your arms because the faster you strip in the line the more fish are taken. And I can guarantee that other anglers will think you are some kind of nut when they see you using this technique. I just ignore them, though, because this is one of the most exciting ways to take steelheads.

As I've mentioned, most steelhead streams, if not all of them, have large tidal basins where they pour into salt water. Even a tiny stream will have a fairly large tidal stretch. And the techniques of taking steelheads from these prime areas are very different from stream to stream. However, in general, your problem in fishing these sections is usually a matter of covering a large amount of water in the most economical way. This almost guarantees that the use of a boat is necessary.

I've never had much luck merely trolling for steelheads, although I've seen hundreds of anglers slowly dragging lures and flies around in tidal waters. I've found that steelheads usually prefer a few limited locations of small size, and that there will be far more fish in a half dozen places than there are in all the rest of the tidal basin put together. This means that the newcomer to a tidal basin should certainly try to get local dope as to where the fish usually hole up. If you can't get someone to loosen up with this information, you are better off spending some time just moving around with your eyes open to see where the local talent is concentrating their fishing effort, rather than merely fishing endless, featureless expanses of open water.

I've found that the very last pools before the river proper starts are usually the finest fishing holes for steelheads in just about every river I've ever fished. I think that the steelheads sort of pause in these pools to get acclimated to the change from tidal surge to river currents. I'd say that most of the first efforts should be spent fishing these pools before you move out into the tidal bays proper.

One of the best techniques to use from a boat is drifting and "mooching." Mooching is a technique borrowed from salmon fishermen. All it amounts to is weighting a bait, letting the bait down to the bottom, and drifting where the wind and tide takes you. As you move along you repeatedly bring the rod tip up and then let it down to the bottom again. This gives bait a noticeable movement in the water and lets you cover a wide swath of water with each drift.

Another method, used where there is a strong tidal surge that makes fast movement of the boat a problem, is "back drifting." Back drifting is also used in strong flowing streams like the Columbia or the Sacramento. In back drifting, the boater drives his boat up to the foot of the tide currents, rapids, or riffles. Then he flips the motor out of gear, letting the motor idle while he back drifts downstream. Then he casts to the foot or break of the current with his terminal rigging set up for drift fishing. He has just enough weight to take the lure or bait down to the bottom so that it taps along on the stones or gravel.

I prefer lures such as the flatfish or cherry bobber, which float, for back drifting. These lures stay up off the bottom and are fairly easy to retrieve in a hurry. The boat is pushed along by the current and the lure fishes a swath of water by trailing out *upstream* from the boat. When the currents lets go of the boat and starts to slow down the drift, the motor is engaged again, the lures or bait retrieved, and another run is made to the top of the heavy current. You can imagine how tricky it is trying to control both fish and boat at the same time that they are in the grips of a strong current. This is an exciting technique but it works for steelheads.

To end up, I'll mention again that fishing the mouths

of tributary creeks and rivers is always a good idea. These
are rallying points for steelheads because the fish pause
here before they make up their minds about entering
these spawning tributaries. The same thing applies to
other, less obvious places.

For instance, a steelhead will usually hit best at the
edges of a run of fast water. They hold and seem to be
in a striking mood when they are at the point where the
character of the stream or tidal basin is changing in some
noticeable way. A rocky stretch of stream that suddenly
churns into a slower, sandy or gravelled stretch will get
the steelies into a feeding mood. They seem to hit best
in tidal waters, just as the tide changes. And it doesn't
seem to matter if the tide is at maximum or minimum,
just as long as it is on the verge of some sort of change.
Other changes are when the clouds part about mid-morn-
ing, and the sun clamps down on the water. When a calm
day becomes windy, it seems to stimulate steelheads on
occasion; or when the windy day suddenly turns calm.
The same is true in the case of rain. The steelhead will
go on a feeding binge just at the start of a rainstorm. Or
the fish will feed faster as a river rises or drops due to
rainstorms.

It is impossible to more than hint at all of the *possibilities for change* in the conditions when you are on any
given steelhead stream. An angler has to be constantly
on the alert for these things. Every steelhead fisherman
sooner or later learns that changing conditions govern
the habits of the steelheads. But few of them can agree
about what exact effect these changes have. The angler
who is most correct in defining the meanings of these
changes, in terms of the fish, is the most consistently successful angler on that particular river. There is no other
way to look at this situation.

13 Women and Steelhead Fishing

The subject of women and steelhead fishing is debatable in most circles. The boys seem to divide up into two groups, those who say that women do not belong on the steelhead streams and those who claim that their women are the finest little steelhead fishermen who ever waded a stream. I think that the true answer lies somewhere between these extremes.

I feel that women, and children for that matter, do belong on the streams with the qualification that the conditions are right for this type of family sport. For instance, I have never, personally, met a woman who is absolutely sold on the subject of steelhead fishing. I don't doubt that such a woman exists, but I haven't met her. However, I have met and fished beside several women who are very competent steelhead practitioners. By this I mean that there is nothing about the techniques of steelhead fishing that can't be mastered by a woman or an intelligent youngster. But there is a great gap between merely being competent with rod and reel and the techniques of lure or bait handling and becoming a consistently successful, practical steelhead fisherman.

As I've repeated time after time in this work, catching the steelheads is the easiest part of the game. And I feel that women and youngsters should be more or less left out of the often rugged job of locating the runs of fish.

There is nothing quite so boring to a young steelhead fisherman as an extended session of water sampling when the fish are hard to find. The youngster will get bored to distraction if he has to fish hour after hour and drive possibly hundreds of miles before a run of fish is located. And while a woman may be able to take the boredom associated with this critical phase of steelhead fishing, I think that they are a hindrance to a man at the streamside. My own wife can throw a fly line with the best of the male talent on any stream. She can use all the equipment associated with the sport to perfection. She isn't the type who has to have knots tied for her, and she doesn't become giddy at the thought of handling a gooey gob of fresh roe or a bait of any kind. But when it comes to hopping from rock to rock or walking on slick streamside rocks or wading on top of mossy stream bottoms, she is not at all efficient.

I have noticed that the vast majority of women also fall down in this category of streamside agility. But this isn't the worst of it. Women just seem to have more native good sense than men. They can see little point in fishing when their fingers are so cold that they feel like they are made of stone. They will give up easily when the rain pelts down on the stream. They cannot see the sense of hanging in there to get that last cast, and then take another half dozen casts; and yet these are features that most dedicated male steelhead fishermen do automatically, as a matter of course.

So I think the place for women and youngsters comes only after the father or husband has located the runs of steelheads. Naturally, if either a woman or youngster wants to get in there and do a share of the searching, I wouldn't stop them—just as long as they didn't slow down this serious phase of steelhead fishing too much. But I do think that the father or husband shouldn't really expect the family to pull an equal share of the burden of searching.

Every time I hear a steelhead fishing father or husband say that his kinfolks don't like steelhead fishing in any way, shape, or form, I'd be willing to bet that either one of two things happened the first few times he took the family steelhead fishing. I believe that it is absolutely impossible for anyone, regardless of age or sex, to dislike a successful introduction to steelhead fishing.

The steelheading father or husband who is stuck with a family that loathes steelhead fishing probably took the wife and child to a convenient pool. He gave each of them one of his old fishing outfits. (I've seen kinfolks of steelhead fishermen trying to fish with a bamboo rod that had the line tied to the end of the pole!) He baited up the hook for them, handed them the old rod and reel, told them to be careful not to fall in the water, *then he took off for the real fishing waters by himself,* or with the boys in the gang. The spouse and child sat alertly for a while. Then they lost interest. Finally, they ignored the whole business. All I can say is what would any other sane person have done under these conditions?

The other possibility is that the father dragged the pair of them out of bed at two hours before sunup, saw to it that they stuffed down a tepid breakfast, and then dragged them half asleep to the edge of a dreary stream.

The rain pelted them for a couple of hours and they suffered because they didn't have adequate rain gear like the old pro was wearing. Then the rain stopped and the cold set in. The line was freezing in the guides and everyone's ears were so cold that you could have knocked them off with a stick. To top this scene off, nobody caught any fish that day.

You'll have to take my word for it that this happens several thousand times each year. I've seen it happen so often—the father or husband stacks the deck on his family when he takes them steelhead fishing—that I hardly even notice it any more. Long ago, when I was much younger and more foolish, I would make a comment or two about this kind of treatment of the little people. I no longer make verbal statements of this type —you can get your ears pinned back for it—but there's nothing stopping me from putting it in print. My own feeling on this matter can be summed up by saying: The wife or scion of the family should be given every conceivable break when they go fishing for steelheads, at least the first few times.

As far as equipment goes, if the family only owns a single good steelhead rig, the beginner should be using this outfit. After all, the old man has years of experience at handling equipment so he's much better able to get at least a bit of efficiency out of older rods and reels that don't come up to standard for steelheading. And I feel that the father or husband who wants his family to join him in his love for the game of steelheading should actually not carry a rod or reel with him at all on the first few days of steelhead fishing when his family goes along. Believe me, these first few sessions of steelhead fishing are critical to the end product of getting the family interested in steelheading.

If the weather is bad, the father or husband should

either postpone this session on the stream in favor of waiting for better weather or he should fork over enough cash to get the family the very best of weather protection gear. This can be a serious drain on the finances, especially in the case of a youngster who is still growing. A pair of waders or hip boots soon gets too small for a growing boy or girl, yet they are just as expensive as the pair the father is wearing. A parka can be bought large so the lad can grow into it. But undergarments meant to defeat cold and wetness are other items that cannot be made to stretch into the years of growth. So I think that the better decision would be postponement rather than fish and be damned, regardless of the weather.

When you add up all of these elements, they come out to the fact that taking the family fishing is rewarding if it is done with a bit of forethought, a healthy amount of money, and a whole lot of patience on the part of the teacher. I feel that there is no other way to do the job of teaching the family to be steelhead addicts than to go about it in this manner.

In the matter of selection of steelhead fishing tackle, I have some very definite ideas. I feel that most steelhead fishermen make a basic mistake when they choose tackle for the rest of the family. Even if money is no object and they get the best for the family, they will usually try to pare down the size of the rod used by the lighter wife, daughter or son. And while a fly fishing family might find it good to get junior or daughter a rod about 6 in. shorter than the father or mother's fly rod, going much farther than this is a mistake. Nothing is more fatiguing than trying to make long casts with a short, limber fly rod. In effect, what you are doing when you try to cast with a soft fly rod or one that is short is to

make up for the lack of built-in strength in the rod
with the muscles of your arm. For instance, I have found
that I can cast a shooting head almost as far with a 7½ ft.
dry fly rod as I can with my 9 ft. steelhead rod. But my
arm feels like someone has been beating on it with a
hammer if I fish with this light outfit for any length of
time.

By the same token, the wife or youngster shouldn't be
saddled with an ultimate distance rod of any kind,
weather it's fly fishing, spinning, or a level wind rig.
Actually, the male fisherman is foolish if he uses these
maximum distance outfits if he doesn't absolutely need
them. For everybody concerned, the best choice in any
steelhead fishing tackle is an average, medium weight and
action rod fitted with a standard model reel. The main
thing the father or husband should try for is quality,
at least as high as he uses when he selects an outfit for
another member of the family.

The subject of rocks and youngsters always comes up
when the kids go along on any fishing trip. A steelhead
trip can be made very dismal for everyone in sight, especially for the rest of the people fishing the streams, if
junior or sister starts skimming nice, flat streamside
stones across the water when the action slows down. And
yet, I've never seen a single case where a youngster was
near a stream, lake, bay, or ocean where they could resist
throwing rocks into, over, and across the water. Rocks,
kids, and water go together like ham and eggs. So the
father should expect this facet whether he is in the immediate area where the youngster is doing his skimming,
or whether he has wandered off up or down the stream.
Nothing can get a family a more chilly reception than
a rock skimming session when there are a lot of other
fishermen nearby. The father should expect this element

to come up sooner or later and take steps to avoid the consequences when it does. Picking a nice, secluded area to fish is much harder than it would seem, so the only other thing he can do is point out the folly of this kind of play where it interferes with other anglers.

I once saw a mother and father allow their son to repeatedly throw large rocks into a riffle and pool where half a dozen men were fishing. At first the guys in the lineup merely grumbled. But when the boy kept up the throwing, one monolithic individual detached himself from the end of the lineup and came trudging over to the family, basking on a sandbar. He asked, "Is that your kid throwing rocks in the water over there?"

The father of the erring youth grinned and said, "It's a public river."

The big bruiser picked the father up and threw him out into the middle of the river. The wife screamed so loud she sounded like a stepped-on cat. A daughter squealed and raced back and forth on the bank. The father finally came gasping to shore. The oversized angler picked up his rod and went back to his fishing. The family left soon after.

I have also seen cases where a father will demand that the youngster not move, talk, or ramble around looking for things under streamside rocks. In every case the youngster was miserable and bored. I think that the subject can be settled by saying that women and children are entitled to sup the joys of steelhead fishing. It's doubtful that they ever will be able to see the point in sharing any of the miseries connected with the sport. But a calm detached look at the whole game of steelheading certainly adds up to good, clean family sport as soon as the details are worked out.

14 Where, When, and Who for Steelheads: California

It is almost impossible to pinpoint a run of steelheads even in a single stream. It is more difficult to try to point to all the rivers that may have fish in them and say which will have steelheads at any given time of the year. In many cases the mouths of certain creeks and small rivers have to be washed out before they can allow the steelheads to run up stream. In a few cases the mouths of some tiny creeks are completely closed off from the upstream stretches by hundreds of yards—in a few cases, even miles of sand; and yet the upstream area has ample water from spring seepage to support a run of steelheads from year to year.

Then again there is always that matter of the condition of the weather at any particular stage of the season. The reasons why a list of dates can never be either adequate or factual are so numerous that it makes little sense to go into them fully. So, the information that I offer in this chapter is to be looked at as the roughest sort of guide to where steelhead runs might be found. I have excerpted the information from various sources. Other odds and ends of information come from my own experience and from that of other individuals who seemed to know what they were talking about. And the rest of the information just arrived on my desk in unknown ways. The one thing that I can say for this listing is that it is as complete as I can make it at the present time. In California I will start at the southern end of the steelhead range, just south of San Francisco Bay. While I realize that there are a few streams farther south that have runs of steelheads from time to time, I will take the Big Sur River as the logical starting point for the south end of the range.

BIG SUR AND CARMEL RIVERS: These two tiny streams are fairly typical of the tiny creeks that purl down out of the Pacific slope mountains every few miles all along the entire coastline. The amount of rain controls the flow in them to such an extent that it would be foolish to make any kind of lengthy trip just to fish them for steelheads. However, if the angler should find himself in the area near them during the winter months from December to February, and if there had been a considerable amount of rain before this time, he would be silly not to try them at least for a couple of hours each. I would say that any time after the first of December you can count on having steelheads in this type of stream.

The following streams also flow into the Pacific south of the Golden Gate. With the exception of the San Lorenzo River, they are all what could be termed late winter streams. For all intents, they are dry when there is no rain. PAJARO RIVER, SOQUEL CREEK, SAN LORENZO RIVER, SCOTT CREEK, PESCADERO CREEK are all streams that are also worth fishing when the season is rainy, after the end of November.

The following streams are located inside of San Francisco Bay. They are extremely erratic producers of steelhead runs and should be more or less ignored by all but local anglers. Their best months are very late winter— January and February—if then: GUADALUPE CREEK, LOS GATOS CREEK, ALAMITOS CREEK, COYOTE CREEK, STEVENS CREEK, SAN FRANCISQUITO CREEK, ALAMEDA CREEK, SAN LORENZO CREEK.

The inland streams that form the upper part of San Francisco Bay and Delta is a huge system of streams, sloughs, and converging water systems. Originally, the San Joaquin River system extended south to the area near the sizable city of Fresno. But dams in this entire watershed have cut the steelhead and salmon runs down to such an extent that they are barely worth trying. The Sacramento River watershed extended, at one time, into the mountains near the California-Oregon border. This drainage was sliced off at Shasta Dam near the city of Redding. This watershed is in much better shape than the San Joaquin, and steelheads still migrate into it in numbers. The NAPA RIVER flows into an arm of San Francisco Bay near the city of Vallejo and is considered a weak producing winter stream. But there are some steelheads in these watersheds after the month of October during most years.

Taking the SAN JOAQUIN RIVER, there is a massive tangle of sloughs near the confluence of the San Joaquin proper and the Sacramento River. Any of these waters probably have some steelheads in them after the month of August, but a fishery of any size has never developed below the city of Tracy. Upstream, the least important steelhead waters are the MERCED RIVER and the STANISLAUS RIVER; the main SAN JOAQUIN RIVER and the TUOLUMNE RIVER will produce, however, for fishermen who know the waters any time after October. But I wouldn't suggest that a trip be made to this area without specific information about a run then in progress.

THE MOKELUMNE RIVER is being worked on by the Department of Fish and Game at the present time in hopes of rebuilding the salmon and steelhead runs that once were massive in this stream. I expect this stream to produce good steelheading by 1968. The CONSUMNES RIVER is definitely a late winter stream. It is dry most of the months before January.

The following streams, all tributary to the Sacramento River, have steelheads after the month of September. Any of them can produce well for the angler who manages to be on them when the steelhead runs are in progress. The SACRAMENTO RIVER—best in the stretch between the cities of Red Bluff and Redding—is active September through February but December and January are best. The AMERICAN RIVER is fishable for a few miles above the state capital city of Sacramento to the Nimbus Dam—same time table as the Sacramento River. The YUBA RIVER flows into the FEATHER RIVER near the city of Marysville, but neither of these streams are rated as top steelhead producers. I have taken steelheads in both of these streams during the month of November when there had been a moderate amount of rain. But I would say that they should have steelheads in them any time after the first of October in a normal year. DEER CREEK, MILL CREEK, ANTELOPE CREEK, AND BATTLE CREEK are all streams that are worth fishing after the first of October in an average year.

The peak months are November through January. (Battle Creek has the famous Coleman fish Hatchery—salmon primarily—on it and is a fine stream of small size.)

The following streams flow into the Pacific north of the Golden Gate. Just about all of the streams south of the mouth of the Eel River are streams that open up to the migrating steelheads after the first heavy rainfalls of the year, normally during November and often not until after Christmas. The peak production years are those that have heavy rainfalls during the months of September and October, then no storms until after the first of the next year. When this happens, the mouths of the streams open up and the steelheads come in by the thousands. Then the receding water traps them in various sections of the streams. These are what steelheaders in California call "Vintage Years." They don't come very often.

The first stream north of the Golden Gate is PAPERMILL CREEK. This is a short stream but it is productive from late October on, especially in the tidal stretches at the far south end of Tomales Bay. SALMON CREEK is a tiny, tidal river that is best from December until February. The RUSSIAN RIVER, GUALALA RIVER, GARCIA RIVER, BRUSH CREEK, ALDER CREEK, GREENWOOD CREEK, NAVARRO RIVER, ALBION RIVER, BIG RIVER, NOYO RIVER, TEN MILE RIVER are all very good winter streams. The first heavy rains normally come during late November or early December and from then on these streams, which form a massive loop system of varied and productive waters that can be covered by an angler in an automobile during a weekend visit, present one of the finest setups available to the steelhead fisherman. I would judge these streams, taken as a complete group, to be the most productive January and February streams in California—if not in the whole steelhead range.

They are all serviced by U.S. Highway 1, and there are plenty of camping, hotel, and motel accommodations available to service any number of anglers.

The MATTOLE RIVER is difficult to reach for the csaual angler who only has a few days to fish. But it is good any time after late November in most years. The road from Fernbridge is the best choice for the angler as of this writing. There are very few accommodations on the Mattole and none on the BEAR RIVER which is a few miles north of the Mattole.

The EEL RIVER is one of those legendary streams that has beckoned to steelheaders for generations. It consistently produces some of the biggest steelheads taken within the continental United States. I explained in another section of the book why it is not the river it once was, but here I'll point out that the Eel River is actually a lengthy system of streams. The best months to fish the Eel are from mid October at the mouth near Fernbridge and then up-stream during the months after mid-November. The VAN DUZEN is a fine, small stream that flows through some of the finest scenery in the world. But the banks of the Van Duzen are brushy with huge redwoods crowding right to the stream's edge in most places. The best months depend on the rainfall. Normally it is best from December on. There are good accommodations all through the area.

The ELK RIVER flows into Humboldt Bay. It is a winter stream, so tiny that you have to look hard just to find it. Best months are January and February. The MAD RIVER is a very fine stream that is easy to get to. It has good to very good runs of steelheads any time after October. LITTLE RIVER is a tidal stream and the best time to fish it, if at all, is January and February. REDWOOD CREEK is a modest stream that has good runs during December until February. It is serviced at the town of Orick and is best in tidal stretches below town.

The KLAMATH RIVER, TRINITY RIVER, SALMON RIVER, SCOTT RIVER is a drainage that covers most of far northern California. I have mentioned this famous drainage extensively in the rest of this work, so I'll only say that the starting date for runs of steelheads is September to late February. In any drainage of this size, you can be assured that there are fish to be had after mid-September. The peak months for the whole drainage are October through December. Heavy rains make fishing more difficult after the first of the new year.

The SMITH RIVER is a unique stream. It has the distinction of being one of the fastest clearing streams in the U.S. This means that even during a considerable rainstorm, the water in the Smith River remains reasonably clear so that you can fish with lures. Even the heaviest storms, which dirty even the Smith River, will only keep this stream discolored for a few days to a week. The Smith River also has the reputation of being a "big fish river" because the average fish taken from it will go larger than most other streams. There are very good accommodations near the mouth of the Smith River with many trailer courts but few camping facilities in the prime stretch up to the junction of the river with U.S. Highway 199. The best months are October to February with a peak around the first of the year. I recommend this river highly.

Who to Contact—California

ANDERSON
The Heidelbert Motel; N. U.S. 99, Ph: EM 5-9931
Army Navy Store; 2975 East, Ph: 365-7497
Anderson Valley News; South & West, Ph: 365-2527

BLUE LAKE
Lindstrand's Store; 410 Railroad Ave., Ph: 668-5768
Chamber of Commerce
Blue Lake Advocate; Railroad Ave., & F., Ph: 668-5758

COTTON WOOD
Paul Abell, Ball's Ferry Resort

EUREKA
Broadway Motel; S. U.S. 101 at 1921 Broadway, Ph: HI 2-5582
El Rancho Motel; Broadway & Henderson, Ph: HI 2-1773
Eureka Inn; 7th & F St., Ph: HI 2-6441
Eureka Travelodge; 4th & B St., Ph: HI 3-6345
Hap's Sporting Goods; 2640 Hall Ave., Ph: 442-9529
Buck's Sporting Goods; 3650 Broadway, Ph: 443-1216
Steelhead Louie, 534 5th, Ph: 443-4340
Chamber of Commerce; 2112 Broadway
Humboldt Standard; 328 F St., Ph: 442-1711

FORTUNA
Maple Leaf Motel; S. U.S. 101, Ph: RA 5-2959
Mission Motel; 819 Main St., Ph: RA 5-2125
Six Rivers Motel; S. U.S. 101, Ph: RA 5-4181
Fortuna Hardware Co.; 1221 Main, Ph: 725-4127
Grunert Sporting Goods; 10th & Main, Ph: 725-2223
Chamber of Commerce
Humboldt Beacon and Advance; 928, Ph: 725-2476

GARBERVILLE
Garberville Motel; S. U.S. 101, Ph: 923-2422
Midway Motel; N. U.S. 101, Ph: 923-2351
White Motel; S. U.S. 101, Ph: 923-2561
Redwood Record

JENNER
Casa Rosa Motel; U.S. 101 Business at 1884 Santa Rosa Ave.,
   Santa Rosa, Ph: LI 2-5225
Ocean Cove Motel; 23255 Coast Highway
Town House Motel; U.S. 101 Business at 2363 Santa Rosa
   Ave., Santa Rosa, Ph: LI 6-4711
De Marco Bait Co., 3014 Coffey Lane, Santa Rosa, Ph: 545-0476
Lou's Sporting Goods; 439 4th, Santa Rosa, Ph: 542-1884
Grant King News & Tackle Shop; 2nd, Guerniville, Ph: 869-2156

KLAMATH
Motel Trees; N. U.S. 101, Ph: HU 2-3152
Panther Creek Lodge; N. U.S. 101, Ph: HU 2-2286
Yale Motel; NE off U.S. 101, Ph: HU 2-2431
Klamath Tackle Shop; Ph: HU 2-3091
Vern's Tackle; Ph: HU 2-3144

ORICK
Moseley's Court; N. U.S. 101, Ph: HU 8-9011
Palm Motel; N. U.S. 101, Ph: HU 8-3431
The Humboldt Times; 1177 Huntington, Crescent City, Ph:
   IN 4-3734

POINT ARENA
City Center Motel; 456 N. State St., Ukiah, Ph: 462-2969
Point Arena Court; Mill and Main St., Ph: TU 2-2068
Redwood Motel; 160 Main St., Ph: TU 2-2005
Anchor Marine Supplies; Noyo, Fort Bragg, Ph: 964-3205
Palace Sport and Hobby Shop; 510 S. State, Ukiah, Ph: 462-
   3348
Ukiak Daily Journal; Ukiah, Ph: 462-2991

REDDING
Bel Air Motel, N. U.S. 99 at 540 N. Market St., Ph: CH 3-
   5291
Casa Blance Hotel & Motel; N. U.S. 99, Ph: CH 1-4661
Redding Travelodge; 1055 N. Market St., Ph: CH 3-4231
Thunderbird Lodge; 1350 Pine St., Ph: CH 3-5422
Butch's Bait, Highway 99 N, Ph: 275-2617
Hinkle's Sporting Goods; 1244 Market, Ph: 243-2214
Vern's Sportshop; 460 Highway 44, Ph: 241-5411
Chamber of Commerce; 1340 Buele, Ph: 243-2541
Redding Record & Searchlight; East and Placer, Ph: 243-2424

SACRAMENTO
Desert Sands Motel; 623 16th St., Ph: HI 4-6430
Los Robles Motor Lodge; 2200 Auburn Boulevard, Ph:
   WA 5-3516
Sands Motel; 2160 Auburn Boulevard, Ph: WA 5-8584
Valley Hi Inn; 5321 Stockton Boulevard, Ph: GL 2-4521
Arden Sports Unlimited; 3121 Arden Way; Ph: 487-8023
Dan's Bait & Tackle Shop; 5200 Franklin Boulevard, Ph:
   451-1772
Fruitridge Bait & Tackle Shop; 4131 Fruitridge Road, Ph:
   456-7506

South Sacramento Sport Shop; 4106 Franklin Boulevard, Ph: 452-7093
Chamber of Commerce; 917 Seventh, Ph: 443-3771
Sacramento Bee; 21 & Q, Ph: 273-2000

SANTA CRUZ
Edgewater Beach Motel; 525 Second St., Ph: GA 3-0440
Palmer House; 820 Third St., Ph: GA 3-2783
Villa Del Mar Motel; 321 Riverside Ave., Ph: GA 3-3445
Johnny's Bike and Sport Shop; 1017 Pacific Ave., Ph: 423-5443
Portola Sportshop; 3301 Portola Drive, Ph: 475-6663
Traders Headquarters; 502 Soquel Ave., Ph: 423-2188
Santa Cruz Sentinel; 125 Church, Ph: 423-4242

SMITH RIVER
Valley View Motel; N. U.S. 101, Ph: HU 7-3352
Curly Redwood Lodge; S. U.S. 101, Crescent City, Ph: IN 4-2137
Surf Hotel; Ocean Drive and H St., Crescent City, Ph: IN 4-2163
Antlers Sporting Goods & Liquors; 840 Front, Crescent City, Ph: IN 4-2790
Mel's Gun Shop; 1040 Pacific, Crescent City, Ph: IN 4-2986
G & G Liquor & Sporting Goods; 285 L, Crescent City, Ph: IN 4-4307
Crescent City American; 381 H, Crescent City, Ph: IN 4-2211

WEAVERVILLE
Hanlon Motel; E. U.S. 299, Ph: 623-8741
Motel Trinity; E. U.S. 299, Ph: 623-3281
Red Mill Motel; W. U.S. 299, Ph: 623-4331
Weekly Trinity Journal

MISCELLANEOUS
Department of Fish and Game; 722 Capitol Ave., Sacramento
Fishing & Hunting News; 2051 J Street, Sacramento, Ph: 444-2852
Oakland Tribune; 13 & Franklin Streets, Oakland, Ph: 273-2000
Pacific Out of Doors: 222 Kearny Street, San Francisco, Ph: 334-0162
Redwood Empire Association; 476 Post St., San Francisco, Ph: GA 1-6554
San Francisco Chronicle; 5th & Mission, San Francisco, Ph: GA 1-1111

First row, left to right: Volunteer, Warwick, Well's Special, Winters, Yellow Jay, Yellow Spinner.

Second row: Black Ghost, Black Marabou, Blue Devil, Gold.

Third row: Gray Ghost, Jersey Minnow, Needabeh, Optic Bucktail.

Fourth row: Scott, Trinity, Wesley, White Marabou.

Fifth row: Yellow Marabou.

Top row, left to right: Brown Hackle, Butcher, Buzz, Cahill, Golden Rod, Gray Hackle Yellow.

Second row: Green Midge, Grizzly Palmer, Imp, Marlow, Midge Black, Orleans Barber.

Third row: Priest, Spider, White Hackle.

Fourth row: Black Nymph, Blue Nymph, Brown and White Nymph, Bug Nymph, Caddis, Freeman Shrimp.

Fifth row: Fur Nymph, Golden Bug Nymph, Gray and Brown Nymph, Gray Bug, Gray Nymph, Olive Nymph.

Sixth row: Red Nymph, Rust Nymph, Wooly Worm, Yellow and Brown Nymph.

Top row, left to right: Boss, Boss Blue, Boss Gray, Boss Orange, Boss Red.

Second row: Boss White, Boss Yellow, Comet, Comet Black, Comet Blue.

Third Row: Comet Brown, Comet Gray, Comet Olive, Comet Orange, Comet Red.

Fourth row: Comet Yellow, Rat-Tail, Razor Back, Razor Back Marabou, Razor Back White.

Fifth row: Razor Back Yellow, Yarn Fly.

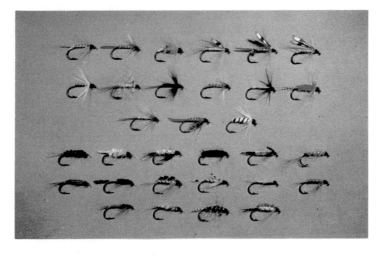

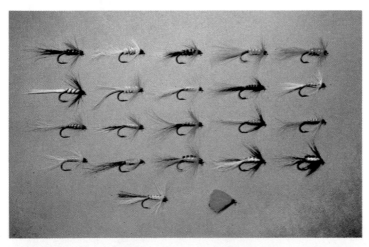

San Francisco Examiner; 3rd & Market, San Francisco, Ph:
  SU 1-2424
U.S. Geological Survey, Federal Center, Denver 2, Colorado
Weekend News; 2633 Ivy Drive, Oakland, Ph: TE 4-3711
Western Outdoors, Box 2027, Newport Beach

15 Where, When, and Who for Steelheads: Oregon and Idaho

The valid information concerning the steelhead streams on the Oregon coast is surprisingly scarce. There are a few rivers such as the Rogue and the North Umpqua that have been made famous by publicity. On these streams there is, if anything, too much information. The rest of these great stream systems have been pretty well ignored by all but the local anglers. Many of the really great streams such as the Nestucca River and the Yaquina are little known to anglers unless they live in Oregon.

The Nestucca, for instance, carries a great deal of pressure from Portland and Salem anglers after the first few rainstorms of winter or late fall. The reason for this is that the streams are a short trip from these population centers —besides being very fine steelhead and salmon streams.

The Rogue and the Umpqua are harder to reach by the mass of anglers who live in Oregon. I'll start the list by dividing the Oregon coastline into three rough sections. The southern section ending at Coos Bay starts at the south at the California-Oregon state line.

The first stream north of the border is the WINCHUCK, a tiny stream that isn't fishable for steelheads until after the first winter rains. Best months are January through March. The CHETCO RIVER is the best stream for steelheads south of the Rogue. It is serviced by the sizable town of Brookings and doesn't have too much fishing pressure. I've taken many steelheads from the Chetco and every fish is above the 8 lb. mark. Best months are January and February. The PISTOL RIVER is a tiny stream during the fall and summer, but after a few rainstorms it has good runs of large fish. The best months are from December through February.

The ROGUE RIVER is good just about any month with the exception of June. Even then, there are many steelheads in the Rogue. The Rogue is a big river, and it is hard to get at for the angler who is depending mainly on his automobile for transportation. To fish the Rogue correctly, you should take a boat upstream from Gold Beach and have them drop you off so you can camp and fish in solitude. The best months are September and October and any month from December through spring.

Just to the north of the mouth of the Rogue River, at Cape Blanco, there are two small streams, the ELK and the SIXES RIVERS. These streams need sizable rains to let the steelheads pass the tidewater stretches. They are brushy-banked streams, but they clear up quickly after a rainstorm and are worth remembering any time during the December and January months when the larger streams in the area are discolored from rainstorms.

The center section of the Oregon coast starts in the south at the Coquille River and extends to the Nestucca River. The streams in this stretch of coast are better serviced by the road system than those farther south, so they are much more attractive to the angler who is working the coast, searching for steelheads. The COQUILLE RIVER discolors badly during winter rainstorms. There are some steelheads taken just above the town of Bandon during November in dry years, but the best months are still December through February on the average year. The COOS RIVER and BAY is much the same as the Coquille. Winter runoffs effect the water violently and local enquiry is essential. There is a run of small steelheads during September and October in the Bay during most years. But most of the local people are fishing for salmon at this time and can't be bothered with the steelheads.

TENMILE CREEK and TENMILE LAKE have runs of steelheads any time after October. These fish follow the silver salmon upstream and their abundance depends on the numbers of salmon. The UMPQUA RIVER has an extremely long tidal lagoon at its mouth at Winchester Bay. The first stream fishing takes place at Sawyers Rapids about 20 miles upstream off Highway 38. Access from the road is controlled by private landowners, and fishing the downstream section of this stream usually requires a boat so you can float the stream. And it had better be a rubber boat because the Umpqua is a rough river in sections. The upstream or NORTH FORK section is reached from Highway 99 (north and south) and the target cities are Glide and Steamboat. The river is fairly hard to reach, but the rewards of taking large fish with a fly (only) during the summer months makes this section of the Umpqua world famous. Some of the river upstream is privately controlled, but much of it up towards Steamboat is on National

Forest property. Best months downstream are November through January; upstream, July and September.

The bulk of the streams in the central coast section of Oregon are winter streams. But either the SUISLAW RIVER, ALSEA RIVER, YAQUINA RIVER, SILETZ RIVER or the NESTUCCA RIVER will have good runs of steelheads any time after the first of November. Most of these rivers have fair to good access roads and they drain mixed agriculture and forest products areas. This is an important point because the extent of forestry or farming activity can change the character of a stream system drastically in even a short period of time. The primary considerations for the angler new to the area of any of these stream systems are access and weather. The best months, generally, are January and February.

Several small streams feed into Tillamook Bay. Of these the TRASK RIVER and the WILSON RIVER support the bulk of the angler attention. But the TILLAMOOK RIVER, KILCHUS RIVER and the MIAMI RIVER are all good streams. They are good streams to consider, even though the access is limited, when big storms make the larger streams hard to fish. They are all best from January through March.

The NEHALEM RIVER has a road that parallels the stream for many miles upstream to Jewel. The best seasons are January through spring.

The COLUMBIA RIVER has never been noted for its steelhead fishing. The river is just too massive. The WILLAMETTE RIVER is also a bit too big for good steelhead fishing, although Portland and Salem anglers are numerous enough on this stream to show at least a few fish, considering the number of anglers on the stream. Better streams, serviced by good roads, are the SANTIAM RIVER, MCKENZIE RIVER as well as the UPPER WILLAMETTE. The McKenzie is best fished from a boat and the Santiam from the banks.

The best seasons are any time from November through February.

Idaho

Even though Idaho is remote from the Pacific Ocean it still offers some fairly good steelhead fishing. The main fishing pressure is concentrated on the rivers that are easy to reach. The best access is to the CLEARWATER RIVER and the SALMON RIVER.

The Clearwater River and its main tributaries have two distinct runs of steelheads. The first is a winter run that starts in February and runs through April. The river system fluctuates wildly during this spring runoff period, so any angler coming in from another state should certainly call ahead and find out how the water situation is. Most of the pressure is by boat fishermen below the dam at the city of Lewiston. But some shore casters fish above the dam.

The fall season starts in November and goes on throughout the winter months. It takes a boat for the best of this fishing, but when the runoff conditions, controlled by heavy freezing in the mountains, are right, this is the best time of year to fish. Oddly enough, the Clearwater lives up to its name and is clear during the deep winter months. The fish are big in this entire drainage, too.

The SALMON RIVER has limited access. It is on the same timetable as the Clearwater. Personally, I feel that the angler would be best advised if he could combine a hunting trip along with his steelhead fishing in the entire Lower Salmon River and Stanley Basin area. This way he's almost certain to take a few steelheads during late September and October, along with a bag of big game. The country is just too hard to penetrate to make it worth while to go into just to fish alone.

Who to Contact—Oregon

ASTORIA
Columbia Motel; 1245 W. Marin Dr., Ph: FA 5-6561
Crest Motel; 2 mi. E. U.S. 30 at 5366 Leif Erickson Dr., Ph: FA 5-3141
Lee City Center Motel; 495 Marine Dr., Ph: FA 5-4211
Sunny Lane Motel; 2 mi. S. U.S. 101, Ph: FA 5-3231
Chamber of Commerce; 339 West Second Avenue

BROOKINGS
Bonn Motel; N. U.S. 101, Ph: 5711
Crest Motel; N. U.S. 101, Ph: 5691
Harbor Supplies; 101 Chetco Avenue, Ph: 469-2993
Leo's Sporthaven Marina; Harbor, Ph: 469-3301
Bill's Tackle Shop; Spruce, Ph: 469-2355
Brooking Harbor Pilot; 503 Chetco Avenue, Ph: 469-2012
The Oregonian Journal; Harris Heights Road, Ph: 469-2545

COOS BAY
Bayshore Motel; N. U.S. 101, Ph: CO 7-4138
Lazy J. Motel; S. U.S. 101, Ph: CO 7-6847
Terrace Motel; S. U.S. 101, Ph: CO 7-6488
Harless Outdoor Store; 1127 S. Broadway, Ph: 267-3311
Penny's Tackle Box; 675 Newport, Ph: 267-4294
Stewarts Sport Shop; 130 N. Broadway, Ph: 267-6318
Chamber of Commerce; 143 W. Commercial, Ph: 267-6519

EUGENE
Eugene Hotel; 222 E. Broadway, Ph: DI 4-1461
Eugene Travelodge; S. U.S. 99W at 540 E. Broadway, Ph: DI 2-1109
Manor Motel; S. U.S. 99W at 599 E. Broadway, Ph: DI 5-2331
The Timbers Motel; 1015 Pearl Street, DI 3-3345
Andy Maxon Tackle Shop; 760 Blair Boulevard, Ph: 344-8061
Jackson's Tackle Shop; 985 6th Avenue W; Ph: 345-3606
Tackle Shack; 769 Highway 99N, Ph: 342-4742
Eugene Register—Guard; 975 High, Ph: 345-1031

GOLD BEACH
Capri Motel; S. U.S. 101, Ph: CH 7-5811
Elliott's Motel; N. U.S. 101, Ph: CH 7-4351
Wright's Motel; S. U.S. 101, Ph: CH 7-5566

Morrie's Outdoor Store; Ph: CH 7-4893
Johnny's Tackle; 555 N. Ellensburg, Ph: CH 7-4204
Curry County Reporter; 140 Caughell Road, Ph: CH 7-2321

IDLEYLD PARK
Idleyld Store
Circle H
Old Kentucky Homes

PORTLAND
Congress Hotel; 1024 SW 6th Avenue, Ph: CA 8-0181
Imperial Hotel; 410 SW Broadway, Ph: CA 8-7221
Ongford Hotel Apts.; 1417 SW 10th Ave., Ph: CA 3-6603
Sheraton Portland Hotel; 1000 NE Multnomah St., Ph: AT 8-6111
Andy & Bax Surplus; 1234 SE Union Ave., Ph: 6-5377
Foster Sporting Goods; 7916 SE Foster Road; Ph: PR 5-6751
Freeway Sporting Goods; 1902 NE Broadway; Ph: AT 1-1177
Gateway Surplus; NE 103rd & Halsey, Ph: 254-7852
Oregon Journal; 1320 SW Broadway, Ph: CA 2-5511
Chamber of Commerce; 1020 SW Front Avenue

REEDSPORT
Fir Grove Motel; S. U.S. 101, Ph: CR 1-2221
Reedsport Motel; S. U.S. 101, Ph: CR 1-2079
Echo Resort; 7 mi. E State 38, Ph: CR 1-2025
Kaufman's Sport Shop; Winchester Bay, Ph: CR 1-3232
Reedsport Outdoor Shop; 2049 Winchester Avenue, Ph:
    CR 1-2311

SALEM
La Vista Motel; S. U.S. Business Route at 2990 S. Commercial
    St. Ph: EM 2-6792
Senator Hotel; 515 Court, Ph: EM 3-4151
Town & Country Motel; S. U.S. 99 Business Route at 2505
    S. Commercial St., Ph: EM 2-9404
Travelers Inn; 3 mi. N. U.S. 99E Business Route at 3230
    N.E. Portland St., Ph: JU 1-2444
Bill Beard Sporting Goods; 372 State, Ph: 363-6042
Four Corners Hardware & Sporting Goods; 155 Lancaster Dr.,
    S.E., Ph: 362-6100
Oregon Journal; 1006 Tild Road, N.D., Ph: 363-7769
Travel Information Dept., Room 101, Highway Building

TILLAMOOK
El Rey Sands Motel; 815 Main Ave., Ph: VI 2-7511
Greenacres Motor Court; N. U.S. 101, Ph: VI 2-2731

Mar-Clair Motel; 11 Main Avenue, Ph: VI 2-7571
Chamber of Commerce; 2105 First Street

MISCELLANEOUS
Oregon State Game Commission; 1634 S.W. Alder St., Portland 8
Oregon Motor Court Association; 729 S.E. Morrison St., Portland 14
U.S. Forest Service, P. O. Box 4137, Portland (maps)
Fishing & Hunting News; 7816 N. Interstate Ave., Portland

Who to Contact—Idaho

BOISE
Lea Bacos Guide Service; P. O. Box 2602

CHALLIS
Abbott Aviation Inc., Ph: TR 9-2231
Round Valley Motel; U.S. 93, Ph: TR 9-2773

LEWISTON
Erb Hardware
Hotel Lewis-Clark
Sacajawea Lodge; 1824 Main St., Ph: SH 3-1575

LOWER STANLEY
Markles Store & Cabins; Highway 93

OROFINO
Riverside Market, Ph: GR 2-5111
Riverside Motel; Highway 9, Ph: GR 2-6511
Snyders; 235 Johnson Avenue, Ph: GR 2-3481
Tom's Flying Service, Ph: GR 2-2682

NORTH FORK
Don L. Smith; P. O. Box 61

SALMON
Twin Peaks Ranch

STANLY
C.A. Gregory Store

MISCELLANEOUS
Idaho Fishing and Hunting Guide; 611 Hays St., Boise
Idaho State Sportsmen Ass'n., P. O. Box 1492, Pocatello
Idaho Tourist Enterprises; 3132 Chinden Avenue, Boise
State of Idaho, Dept. Commerce & Development, State House, Boise

16 Where, When, and Who for Steelheads: Washington

The angler who fishes the state of Washington—at least during the winter months from December through April —is very lucky because the Washington State Game Department has done a good deal of his job of locating the runs of steelheads in the stream for him. Washington State has a unique system of punch cards that each angler is required by law to carry and mark whenever he takes a steelhead from any stream in the state. This punch card is then sent into the game department for summing up the total catch during any given season.

These all important lists, compiled by the game department, are then published for the public as well as for the management of the fisheries on each stream. They are the most complete summation that I have been able to find for any state or province. I have a thick file of information on the 150 or so streams that have runs of steelheads in

Washington, but much of this information has become dated because of changes in the watershed of certain streams—such as new dams, extensive lumbering or mining operations, stream diversions, etc. I have decided to merely report the major lists from the game department's, "Game Bulletin," the monthly news magazine published by the department for the members of the game service and the public. I have chosen from various yearly lists that I have on hand with the intent of giving a well-rounded selection of statistics concerning groups of streams as well as definite information as to when and where the fishing has been best in the past.

List No. 1 contains the game department's compilation of streams and their yield for three specific years—1955, 1958, and 1960. The catch statistics do not take into account the number of fish caught and released by anglers. These catch statistics are also "Total Estimated Catch Statistics." The number of cards that were actually turned in properly marked have been multiplied by the department fisheries managers in order to come up with the more realistic estimate. This estimate is as correct as the game department can make it because many anglers foolishly do not mark or turn in their cards religiously as they certainly should.

Also, on list No. 1 the reader will notice that some streams were dropped from the lists and others added. This is due to the fact that the reported catch was either small or non-existent during certain years. I have included a few streams on the game department lists that have no figures in order that the list of possibilities might be more complete as regards the fact that steelheads can run into these particular streams even if nobody ever catches a fish from them or neglects to send in his punch card if he does mark the card after fishing.

List No. 1
Washington Steelhead Streams

STREAMS	1955 EST. CATCH	BEST MONTH	1958 EST. CATCH	BEST MONTH	1960 EST. CATCH	BEST MONTH
Abernathy Cr.	18	Jan.	—	—	—	—
Bear R.	82	Jan.	—	—	—	—
Big Beef Cr.	—	—	172	Feb.	305	Jan.
Big Skookum Cr.	No reports					
Big White Salmon R.	43	Apr.	—	—	—	—
Black R.	No reports					
Bogachiel R.	1292	Jan.	645	Mar.	1519	Mar.
Calawah R.	192	Jan.	—	—	249	Feb.
Canyon Cr.	490	Feb.	172	Jan.	189	Feb.
Carbon R.	422	Jan.	545	Jan.	410	Dec.
Cedar Cr. (Clark Co.)	39	Jan.	—	—	—	—
Cedar R. (King Co.)	479	Feb.	318	Jan.	218	Feb.
Chehalis R.	5044	Dec.	7695	Jan.	4313	Dec.
Chinook R.	No reports					
Chuckanut R.	No reports					
Cispus R.	57	Mar.	—	—	—	—
Clallam R.	156	Jan.	—	—	—	—
Clearwater R.	220	Jan.	—	—	221	Feb.
Cloquallum Cr.	160	Jan.	—	—	—	—
Columbia R.	3699	Dec.	7736	Jan.	9274	Dec.

Stream						
Coulter Cr.	28	Dec./Feb.				
Coweeman R.	163	Jan.	286	Jan.	1125	Feb.
Cowlitz R.	8048	Jan.	9448	Mar.	11,075	Dec.
Dakota Cr.	11	Feb.	—	—	—	—
Deep Cr. (Clallam Co.)	131	Feb.	109	Feb.	129	Dec.
Deep R.	No reports					
Dewatto Cr.	135	Feb.	145	Jan.	241	Jan.
Dickey R.	11	Feb.	—	—	209	Feb.
Dosewallips R.	330	Mar.	1498	Jan.	916	Feb.
Drano Lake	No reports					
Duckabush R.	153	Feb.	1203	Jan.	659	Feb.
Duncan Cr.	No reports					
Dungeness R.	1087	Apr.	1925	Jan.	1652	Apr.
Du Wamish R.	39	Dec.				
Eagle Cr.	No reports					
East Twin R.	82	Dec.	154	Feb.	—	—
Elochoman R.	841	Jan.	1761	Jan.	1234	Dec.
Elk R.	No reports					
Elwha R.	1179	Apr.	1761	Jan.	1389	Mar.
Entiat R.	No reports					
Fisher Slough	No reports					
Germany Cr.	57	Jan.	—	—	—	—
Goldsborough	58	Jan.	—	—	—	—
Grande Ronde R.	1466	Jan.	917	Mar.	1214	Mar.
Green R.	11,101	Jan.	11,381	Jan.	11,774	Jan.
Hamilton Cr.	99	Mar.	118	Jan.	225	Apr.
Hamma Hamma R.	18	Jan.	195	Jan.	185	Feb.

STREAMS	1955 EST. CATCH	BEST MONTH	1958 EST. CATCH	BEST MONTH	1960 EST. CATCH	BEST MONTH
Hoh R.	1754	Jan.	1090	Feb.	1447	Jan.
Hoko R.	671	Dec.	195	Jan.	426	Dec.
Hoquiam R.	145	Feb.	209	Feb.	—	—
Humptulips R.	4491	Jan.	11,404	Jan.	6231	Feb.
Jim Cr.	99	Feb.	—	—	—	—
Johns R.	3	Feb.	122	Dec./Feb.	—	—
Jorsted Cr.	No reports		1271	Jan.	2709	Feb.
Kalama R.	1150	Apr.	—	—	—	—
Kennedy Cr.	11	Jan.	105	Apr.	309	Apr.
Klickitat R.	163	Apr.	—	—	—	—
Lewis R.	650	Jan.	—	—	313	Jan.
No. Fk. Lewis R.	128	Mar.	1952	Dec.	2911	Dec.
E. Fk. Lewis R.	1686	Jan.	—	—	—	—
E. Fk. Lewis R.	No reports		200	Dec.	249	Jan.
Little White Salmon R.	39	Jan./Feb.	—	—	157	Feb.
Lyre R.	206	Dec.	—	—	197	Dec.
McDonald Cr.	—	—	—	—	—	—
Methow R.	21	Dec.	172	Mar.	—	—
Mill Cr. (Cowlitz Co.)	14	Jan.	145	Jan./Feb.		
Mill Cr. (Walla Walla Co.)	17	Mar.				
Mission Cr.	17	Feb.				
Moclips R.	No reports					
Morse Cr.	58	Dec.			273	Feb.
Naselle R.	976	Dec.	2470	Jan.	2243	Dec.

River						
Nemah R. (all forks)	312	Dec.	372	Jan.	161	Feb.
Newaukum R.	156	Feb.	—	—	277	Feb.
Nisqually R.	4597	Jan.	3715	Mar.	3529	Mar.
Nooksack R. (all forks)	2503	Jan.	1489	Mar.	1061	Feb.
North R.	496	Dec.	1053	Jan.	322	Dec.
Ozette R.	3	Jan.	—	—	—	—
Palix R. (all forks)	103	Jan.	—	—	—	—
Percival Cr.	82	Feb.	118	Feb.	108	Feb.
Pilchuck Cr.	238	Jan.	994	Jan.	1013	Feb.
Pilchuck R.	1722	Feb.	7954	Jan.	8832	Jan.
Puyallup R.	13,351	Jan.	318	Feb.	583	Dec.
Pysht R.	309	Jan.	535	Mar.	454	Jan.
Queets R.	1040	Jan.	—	—	—	—
Quilcene R.	46	Jan.	1248	Mar.	997	Jan.
Quillayute R.	277	Mar.	1112	Feb.	647	Dec.
Quinault R.	905	Dec.	—	—	—	—
Raft R.	7	Dec./Feb.	250	Jan.	116	Feb.
Raging R.	366	Feb.	—	—	—	—
Rock Cr.	3	Apr.	241	Jan.	336	Feb.
Salmon Cr. (Clark Co.)	522	Jan.	—	—	—	—
Salmon Cr. (Pacific Co.)	No reports					
Salt Cr.	85	Feb.	413	Jan.	679	Feb.
Samish R.	1360	Dec.	2265	Jan.	1889	Jan.
Sammamish R.	838	Jan.	831	Jan.	1117	Jan.
Satsop R.	1988	Jan.	817	Mar.	876	Jan.
Sauk R.	944	Feb.	817	Feb.	1057	Feb.
Sekiu R.	121	Jan.	—	—	108	Feb.

STREAMS	1955 EST. CATCH	BEST MONTH	1958 EST. CATCH	BEST MONTH	1960 EST. CATCH	BEST MONTH
Skagit	10,284	Jan.	10,764	Mar.	18,568	Jan.
Skamokawa Cr.	18	Jan.	—	—	—	—
Skokomish R.	731	Feb.	617	Mar.	808	Feb.
Skookumchuck R.	404	Mar.	422	Feb.	185	Feb.
Skykomish R.	5495	Jan.	4485	Jan.	3811	Jan.
Smith R.	99	Jan.	263	Feb.	213	Jan.
Snake R.	4019	Jan.	2806	Dec.	4490	Dec.
Snow Cr.	82	Feb.	—	—	—	—
Snohomish R.	3820	Jan.	5121	Jan.	4076	Jan.
Snoqualmie R.	3234	Jan.	3409	Jan.	2159	Feb.
Soleduck R. (Sol Duk R.)	1807	Jan.	1707	Jan.	1934	Feb.
Squalicum Cr.	35	Dec.	—	—	—	—
Stillaguamish R.	2233	Jan.	1198	Mar.	1355	Feb.
N. Fk. Stillaguamish R.	1022	Jan.	1026	Feb.	117	Feb.
S. Fk. Stillaguamish R.	277	Jan.	—	—	338	Jan.
Stuck R.	593	Mar.	—	—	—	—
Suez R.	46	Jan.	—	—	—	—
Suiattle R.	3	Feb.	—	—	—	—
Sultan R.	121	Feb.	191	Jan.	—	—
Tahuya R.	273	Feb.	—	—	350	Feb.
Tilton R.	596	Jan.	295	Mar.	478	Mar.
Tolt R.	941	Dec.	731	Jan.	583	Feb.
Touchet R.	89	Mar.	372	Mar.	121	Feb.
Toutle R.	3056	Jan.	2819	Mar.	4185	Feb.

Tucannon R.	458	Feb.	1149	Mar.	410	Feb.
Union R.	319	Feb.	—	—	442	Jan.
Lk. Union Ship Canal	135	Jan.	191	Jan./Feb.	756	Jan.
Walla Walla R.	1083	Mar.	1852	Mar.	1306	Dec.
Wallace R.	266	Feb.	113	Dec.	197	Feb.
Lk. Washington	192	Jan.	—	—	—	—
Washougal R.	838	Apr.	794	Jan.	2866	Feb.
Wenatchee R.	390	Dec.	926	Dec.	518	Dec.
West Twin R.	50	Feb.	—	—	—	—
Whatcom Cr.	57	Mar.	—	—	—	—
White R. (Stuck)	124	Feb.	295	Dec.	305	Mar.
Willapa R.	1548	Jan.	2981	Jan.	1704	Jan.
Williams Cr.	3	Jan.	—	—	—	—
Wind R.	337	Jan.	113	Jan.	197	Apr.
Wishkah R.	163	Jan.	236	Feb.	165	Feb.
Woodard Cr.	7	Mar.	—	—	—	—
Wynooche R.	1928	Jan.	890	Mar.	800	Feb.
Yakima R.	437	Mar.	1044	Mar.	1057	Feb.
Yellow Hawk Cr.	7	Jan./Mar.	—	—	—	—

List No. 2 is another game department compilation for several years in a row—from 1955 through 1961. It is the "Top Twenty-Five Steelhead Streams" of Washington State. There are actually almost 40 names on this list because some rivers change place on this popularity poll of streams. The reason that I am including this list is so the reader has a chance to place his choice with the leading producers, everything else being equal. However, I'd like to point out one very important thing about all of these statistics: *They do not indicate exactly why it is that a river comes out in the top ten or twenty-five.*

For instance, in nearly every case, the streams in the top ten on these lists have two things in common. They have very good highway access for many miles of their length; and they are usually located near dense population centers. This would indicate that these two factors are very important when it comes to the running up of good seasonal catch scores. If the reader will get out a highway map of the state of Washington I will point out why this is so.

Most of the population in the state of Washington is located around Puget Sound. The cities from Bellingham through Everett, Seattle, and down to Olympia contain well over half of the population of the entire state. There is another pocket of population at Hoquiam and Aberdeen, and except for a few others, this is it at the present time for Washington as far as population goes.

If we look at the map where the three top rivers are located, checking with list No. 2, we come up with three basic rivers: the Skagit which could be considered the top producer, the Green, and the Cowlitz. Checking with the road and river map you'll find that the Skagit is very reasonably reached from the vast population centers of Bellingham-Everett-Seattle-Tacoma. Also, the river is both reasonably long and a fine road parallels it for many miles. The Green River flows right through the main city of Seattle. Not only that, but it is an extensive stream that drains a large watershed, and it is well serviced by many road systems through both valley and mountain sections. The Cowlitz River is readily accessible from Portland, Oregon, Vancouver, Washington, as well as from Olympia-Tacoma-Seattle. It is serviced by the main highways 99, 5, and 12H. It is also a long stream.

If the reader will keep these facts of location and population density in mind as he looks over these lists he will be better able to choose from among the streams listed in any form. Many of the streams on the west coast of the Olympic Peninsula, if they were located where the Green River is, would certainly rate much higher on these lists. For instance, one of my own favorite streams in all of Washington is the Hoh River which drains south out of Olympic National Park. This river is handicapped by the fact that it is serviced by a rough road along the north bank of the stream for only about 20 miles upstream from where Highway 101 crosses the stream just before it enters the Pacific Ocean. The Hoh is particularly good during the colder months because it tends to run clear and strong because it has its source in the glacier section of the Olympic Park. During the warmer fall and summer months the Hoh is not as inviting for a serious steelheader because the melt-off from the extensive snow and glacier fields tends to milk up the water. But once the high country starts to freeze, the Hoh is probably one of the finest steelhead streams anywhere in the world. The same situation exists with other streams in this prolific area of Washington. The Queets River, which enters the Pacific

List No. 2
Washington's Top Twenty-Five Steelhead Streams

STREAM	54-55	55-56	56-57	57-58	58-59	59-60	60-61
Bagachiel	24	—	—	—	—	22	—
Checalis	6	6	7	7	7	9	12
Columbia	11	16	18	6	6	4	6
Cowlitz	4	4	3	4	4	3	3
Dosewallips	—	—	—	23	—	—	—
Dungeness	—	19	15	18	25	21	13
Elwah	25	—	—	—	—	25	—
Elokomin	—	—	25	20	18	—	—
Grays	22	—	21	—	—	—	—
Green	2	3	4	2	2	2	2
Hoh	20	17	22	—	—	23	22
Humptulips	8	7	5	1	3	6	10
Kalama	—	—	—	25	—	15	17
E. Fork Lewis	15	13	12	17	15	13	11
Naselle	—	14	14	15	16	16	—
Nisqually	7	10	9	10	13	12	14
Nooksack	14	12	—	24	24	—	—
North	—	—	—	22	—	—	—
Pilchuck	—	—	23	—	19	—	19
Puyallup	1	2	2	5	5	5	8
Quillayute	—	22	—	—	—	—	—
Samish	23	21	19	16	12	19	15
Sammamish	—	24	—	—	—	—	23

River							
Satsop	—	—	21	—	21	25	17
Sauk	24	—	—	—	—	—	—
Skagit	1	1	10	3	1	1	3
Skykomish	4	11	23	9	6	5	5
Skykomish	—	—	20	—	17	—	—
Sol Duc	20	18	9	21	—	19	19
Snake	5	7	11	14	—	—	9
Snoqualmie	18	17	8	11	8	9	12
Snohomish	9	10	—	8	10	8	10
Stillaguamish	21	24	—	—	—	20	16
N. Fk. Stillaguamish	25	—	14	—	—	—	—
Toutle	16	9	22	12	11	11	13
Walla Walla	7	14	—	—	16	—	—
Washougal	—	—	17	19	—	—	—
Willapa	—	20	—	13	13	15	21
Wynooche	—	—	—	—	24	23	18

Ocean only a few miles south of the Hoh River, would probably be among the top ten rivers in the state if it were serviced by better roads and located near population centers, such as the top three rivers in Washington.

This does not mean, by any stretch of the imagination, that the Green, Skagit, or Cowlitz are not fine, productive streams. Far from it, they are among the best in the entire range. But I do think that the reader should keep the three factors of proximity to population centers, access by road, and length of the stream in mind when he sits down to choose a stream to fish.

List No. 3 is a short, general list compiled from the same punch card system. I am including it to indicate very roughly when the angler should think about fishing Washington streams for steelheads. If you'll notice from list No. 3 as well as the other lists included in this chapter, you can fairly well tell the months that had just the right amount of rainfall by merely looking at the dates when most fish are being caught.

Washington is a very rainy area, and the residents are more used to downpours than are most people in other areas of the country. However, very probably the milder, dryer years are those where the percentage of take is spread over a longer period. This would very likely be the case for 1958–1959 in list No. 3. But rainfall must have washed out a lot of the angling activity sometime around February 1 during the 1960–61 season. I don't know these things for a fact, but I think that this would be a fair guess for what happened that season. Of course, this list is very broad and is included here merely as the roughest sort of guide to the best seasons in Washington steelhead fishing.

List No. 3
Washington Streams—Best Months To Fish

1960-1961 Winter Season:

December	43,371	36.0%
January	32,981	28.0%
February	15,709	13.3%
March	18,304	15.5%
April	8,385	7.1%

1959-1960 Winter Season:

December	32,309	21.79%
January	41,923	27.85%
February	40,216	27.15%
March	24,920	16.81%
April	9,511	6.41%

1958-1959 Winter Season:

December	31,184	24.64%
January	35,484	28.04%
February	29,298	23.15%
March	22,795	18.01%
April	7,769	6.14%

Who to Contact—Washington

ABERDEEN
City Center Motel; 410 W. Wishkah St., Ph: LE 2-3153
Flamingo Motel; 1120 E. Wishkah St., Ph: LE 2-4103
Morch Hotel; Heron and K Streets, Ph: LE 2-3500
Smiley's Motel; 600 E. Wishkah St., Ph: LE 2-3813

BELLINGHAM
City Center Motel; 2419 Elm St., Ph: RE 3-2330
Doric Bellingham Hotel; 119 N. Commercial St., Ph: RE 4-4400
Leopold Hotel & Motor Inn; 1224 Cornwall Ave., Ph: RE 3-3500
H & H Sporting Good Co.; 1322 Commercial, Ph: 733-2050
Yaeger's Shopping Center; 3101 Morthwest Ave., Ph: 733-1080
The Bellingham Herald; Herald Building, Ph: 734-3900
Chamber of Commerce, Herald Building, Ph: 734-1330

FORKS
Forks Motel; S. U.S. 101, Ph: FR 4-2161
Praire Motel; S. U.S. 101, Ph: FR 4-2581
Thunders Motel; 10 mi. W on Mora Road, Ph: FR 4-2902

KELSO
Cloverleaf Motel; 1015 Allen St., Ph: 393-5387
Crest Chalet Motel; 1000 N. 12th Street, Ph: 393-4180
Veys Motel; N. U.S. 99, Ph: 393-35380
Bill's Gun Store; 115 S. Pacific, Ph: 393-3131
Kelso Western Auto Supply, 3rd and Oak, Ph: 395-1380
Ralph's Sport Shop, 211 Allen, Ph: 393-9923
Chamber of Commerce; 1563 Olympia Way, Longview, Ph: 423-8400
Longview Daily News; 12 and Broadway, Longview, Ph: 425-1600

HOQUIAM
Kerns Motel; E. U.S. 101 at 2933 Simpson Ave., Ph: GE 8-1280
Sandstone Motel; off U.S. 410 at 2424 Aberdeen Ave., Ph: 8-4160
Stoken Motel; N. U.S. 101 at 504 Perry Ave., GE 8-4300

QUINAULT
Lake Quinault Lodge, Ph: 2351
Rain Forest Motel; S. Shore Road, Ph: 2271

SEATTLE
Exposition Travelodge; 6th Ave., North at John, Ph: MA 3-2600
Holiday Resort Motel; 19250 Aurora Ave., Ph: LI 2-2760
Tropics Motor Hotel; 225 Aurora Ave., Ph: MA 4-6789
Vance Motor Hotel; 620 Stewart St., Ph: MA 3-2700
Ace Sporting Goods; 13 Mercer, Ph: AT 4-9976
Linc's Tackle & Marine Shop; Rainier S. & S. King, Ph: EA 2-1555
Seattle Fishing Tackle Inc.; 608 2nd, Ph: MA 4-5834
World Fish & Sporting Gear; 2310 E. Union; Ph: 3-9651
Chamber of Commerce; 215 Columbia, Ph: MA 2-5060
Seattle Post; 6th & Wall, Ph: MA 2-2000
Seattle Times; Fairview N. & John, Ph: MA 2-0300

SEQUIM
Silver Sands Resort; 3 mi. E. U.S. 101; Ph: MU 3-4050
Triangle Motel; E. U.S. 101, Ph: MU 3-5950

TACOMA
City Center Motel; 1521 6th Ave., Ph: BR 2-3536
Fountain Motel; 9915 S. Tacoma Way, Ph: JU 8-4262
Tacoma Travelodge; 2512 Pacific Ave., Ph: FU 3-3557
Winthrop Western Motel; 9th & Broadway, BR 2-2141
Bentz Fly & Tackle Co.; 5427 Pacific, Ph: GR 2-3244
Les Davis Fishing Tackle; 1565 Center, Ph: BR 2-0515
Tacoma Sporting Goods; 5915 6th Ave., Ph: SK 9-0200
Parkland Sports Center; 1122 Pacific Ave., Ph: LE 7-5677
Chamber of Commerce, Winthrop Motel, Ph: MA 7-2175
Tacoma News Tribune; 711 St. Helens, Ph: BR 2-2121
Tacoma Daily Index; 726 Pacific, Ph: 7-4853

VANCOUVER
City Center Motel; 601 Broadway, Ph: OX 3-3668
Fort Motel; 500 E. 13th St., Ph: OX 4-3327
Red Top Lodge Motel; 4 mi. N. U.S. 99, Ph: OG 3-4759
Webb's Stagecoach Inn; 5 mi. N. U.S. 99, Ph: OX 3-5829
Archer's Hiway Garage & Sporting Goods; 8724 NE Highway
  99, Ph: OX 3-8481
Coast to Coast Stores; 711 Main, Ph: OX 4-4921
Sporting Goods; 3001 Fourth Plain Blvd., Ph: OX 5-7372
Jaffe's Sporting Goods; 1901 Main, Ph: 693-2661
Chamber of Commerce; 817 Washington, Ph: OX 4-2588
The Columbian; W 8th & Grant, Ph: OX 4-3391

EVERETT
Everett Travelodge; 3030 Broadway, Ph: AL 9-6141
Monte Cristo Hotel; 1507 Wall St., Ph: AL 2-1151
Topper Motel; 1030 Broadway, Ph: AL 9-3151
Bob's Sporting Goods; 1917 Broadway, Ph: 9-3056
Stones Fishing Tackle; 1523 Walnut, Ph: AL 2-0271
Chamber of Commerce; 2532 Wetmore, Ph: AL 2-5106
Everett Daily Herald; Grand & California, Ph: AL 9-5151
Everett Enterprises; 4824 Evergreen Way, AL 9-6550

MISCELLANEOUS
State Dept. of Fisheries, 4015 20th Ave., West, Seattle
Department of Game; 509 Fairview Avenue North, Seattle 9
State Resort Association, 2100 Fifth Avenue, Seattle
Fishing & Hunting News: 1500 Westlake Ave., N., Seattle
Fishing & Hunting News: N. 2012 Ruby St., Spokane

17 Where, When, and Who for Steelheads: British Columbia and Alaska

To the stateside angler used to crowded streams and limited amounts of angling room, the first impressions of the stream fishing in British Columbia are all but overpowering. The number and size of the streams in this gifted province are truly monumental in scope. But there is a very important fly in this ointment of plenty.

Before the angler is in British Columbia for very long he will find out one important detail that isn't pointed out to him in the literature from chambers of commerce: The majority of prime steelheading waters are impossible to get to with ease. Many fine streams that would support thousands of angling days each year if they were located in the United States are so hard to get to in British Columbia that few, if any, anglers ever wet a line in them. For all intents, these streams are in the same virginal state that they enjoyed when only the Indians fished them. About the only thing that has affected them at all is the lumbering and mining industries. Those streams that are easy to get to and which contain runs of steelheads are well attended by both Canadian and American anglers in fairly large numbers. I am stressing these points because so many anglers who make the trek north from the states seem disappointed when they find conditions on easy-to-reach waters not much different than those they are used to at home.

However, there are plenty of fine streams to be fished with relative ease and with at least a measure of virginity. The most logical place to start the list of British Columbia streams is on Vancouver Island, and the most logical place on the island to start the enumeration is at the capital city of Victoria.

A map will show that Victoria is located at the south eastern tip of Vancouver Island. This particular spot is also the natural dividing point between what the natives consider their "summer steelhead streams" and their "winter steelhead streams." In general, this local terminology is basically correct. But it must be remembered that these are northern waters. They are located in a very damp area and even the smallest streams of only a few miles in length usually have a very good head of water in them at all times of the year. As I've stated before, steelheads cannot read, and some steelheads will be found in just about any of the streams mentioned at all times and season of the year.

Some west coast streams on Vancouver Island that are good during the summer months, located on the Pacific or Juan de Fuca side of the island, are easily reached by good roads. You can expect to take fish from 6 lbs. to about 14 lbs. from the STAMP, ASH and NITINAT. The SAN JUAN, HARRIS CREEK, SOOKE and JORDAN are also west coast streams that are not only fine producers, but they are accessible to the auto angler during the summer months.

The streams reached from the east coast road north from Victoria are generally considered later streams. But the KOKSILAH RIVER is rated as good spring and fall as well as during the winter months from December through February. This river is 22 miles long and is reached through the town of Duncan. This same town services the great COWICHAN RIVER, rated by most anglers as the most consistent steelhead stream on the island. The Cowichan is 28 miles long and can be reached by many different routes, including the Lake Cowichan Road, Gibbons Road, Skutz Falls Road and other service roads. It is a large, deep river with a lot of water and power.

The CHEMAINUS RIVER can be a violent river when in flood. It has a pastoral quality about it that I like, but it muddies up fast with any amount of rain. It is 32 miles long and is rated not very productive. It is a mid-winter river and the access road along the south bank is best. The NANAIMO RIVER runs through a deep gorge where the main highway crosses it, but a good access road leads upstream. The best months are January through March. The BIG and LITTLE QUALICUM RIVERS have very good reputations in spite of the fact that they are only seven and eight miles long respectively. The names have little to do with their size. Both have good accessibility. They have steelheads in them for many months of the year with January through May the best.

A note about CHINA CREEK is worth mentioning. My notes show that this stream, 12 miles long, has runs of steelheads from February through April. It is located seven miles southeast of Alberni. It can be reached out of

Alberni on a gravel road. NAHMINT LAKE has steelheads in early spring and fall, reached from Sproat Lake. The PACHENA RIVER, SARITA RIVER, SOMASS RIVER, TAYLOR RIVER are all May to July rivers according to notes from the fish and game departments.

The city of Parksville, north of Nanaimo, services anglers fishing the ENGLISHMAN'S RIVER. This 19 mile-long stream is a beautiful piece of water, small but clear running even in storms and has runs of steelheads spring and fall as well as mid-January to March. The OYSTER RIVER deserves a special mention as a fly fisherman's stream. March, June, August, and September are prime months for this stream. The PUNTLEDGE RIVER, TSABLE RIVER and COURTENAY RIVER are all good fall and deep winter streams.

There are certainly no lack of accommodations at the CAMPBELL RIVER, but I personally prefer fishing a bit farther north during the months from November through March in the SALMON RIVER or the WHITE RIVER, where the east coast road more or less peters out at the present time. There are plans to open up a road all the way to Englewood at Alert Bay, and this would be good news because fishing seems to get better on the island the farther north you are able to go.

Other streams worth mentioning, though they by no means complete the list of waters just on Vancouver Island, are the IRON RIVER, fished year around; the QUINSAM RIVER, best fished from December to March and rated among the top steelhead rivers on the coast; and QUINSAM LAKE which has steelheads in March and April.

The Port Hardy area has a half dozen streams, but it is hard to reach for the casual angler. The KEOGH RIVER season on steelheads is November to April; QUATSIE RIVER, December to April; TSULQUATE RIVER, December to April; CLUXEWE RIVER, December to April. The MARBLE RIVER is special because it has a summer run as well as a winter run; November to March winter run.

I am not going to attempt to give anything like a comprehensive coverage of the mainland British Columbia streams. There are literally thousands of streams in this vast area and if you look at a map of the province you will see that there are no roads worth mentioning for about 400 or 500 miles above Bliss Landing, about 100 miles above Vancouver. I'll just skip around giving general area information as it comes to me from the various sources.

The most accessible areas are Burrard Inlet, Howe Sound, Sechelt Peninsula, Pender Harbor, and Sechelt Inlet. The INDIAN RIVER, at the head of the north arm of Burrard Inlet, has good, early spring steelheading. Access is by logging road. In Howe Sound, POTLATCH CREEK is an early spring stream rated as fair for steelheads. It is a short stream reached by water taxi and private boat with the best months being April and May. MCNAB CREEK has a good March and April run of large steelies in the 18 lb. to 20 lb. class. There is good access on old overgrown logging roads for several miles. Camping is good here. RAINY RIVER is the same as McNab Creek. It enters the sound at Port Mellon and has accommodations at Gibsons.

Over 50 miles of road service Sechelt Peninsula. The spring months are best on CHASTER CREEK at Gower Point but the fishing is inclined to be spotty. ROBERTS CREEK is another spring stream. It is serviced at Roberts Creek and no boats are required. The village of Wilson services MISSION CREEK and you can fish for almost five miles on this stream. It is an early spring stream with good access.

Sechelt Inlet has a few streams. There is boat access to CARLSON CREEK out of Porpoise Bay. This is another early spring stream. The TZOONIE RIVER can be reached by air or by boat from Porpoise Bay. This is not only an early spring stream but it has a good run of winter fish that run to larger sizes. There are no accommodations here but you can camp and there are several miles of good water. The SQUAMISH RIVER is well attended by direct road from Vancouver and is a favorite, especially in the winter months. This large stream hosts steelheads in fair quantity all but during the summer months. The town of Squamish services it at the head of Howe Sound.

Rivers such as the TOBA RIVER at the head of Toba Inlet, the SOUTHGATE RIVER and HOMATHKO RIVERS flowing into Bute Inlet, the KLINAKLINI RIVER in Knoght Inlet, and any of half a thousand other streams of varying size would give any angler a lifetime of steelheading just on this part of the British Columbia coastline. But they are all difficult to reach unless the angler has unlimited time. The BELLA COOLA run of large steelheads is typical. This stream flows into the North Bentinck Arm of the Burke Channel. A run of steelheads regularly occurs from October on in the Bella Coola, but mostly it goes unnoticed by the angling population. A road through Tweedsmuir Provincial Park has been completed to the mouth of the Bella Coola but the weekly boat from Vancouver is the most practical way to reach this area. The best months are January through April, and it isn't difficult for the angler on the stream at this time to take easy limits. But this stream, like most others that are isolated from the general fishing public, will have to wait for better access before it takes its rightful place among the great steelheading waters of the continent.

No steelhead book would be complete without a mention of the KISPIOX RIVER. But when I say that this river is just a key focusing point for fishing the several fine rivers in this area I mean that the BULKELEY and BABINE are also included on the timetable as well. Mid-August through

October is the time to be on these streams. There are fresh run steelheads throughout this entire Skeena River drainage system, but this is the best time for the weather and for water conditions. There is no getting around a river system where you can take 20 lb. steelheads on a fly during the month of August. The only drawback is the time it takes an American angler to get this far into north country. The town of New Hazelton services this system.

The THOMPSON RIVER has been mentioned in some detail in other parts of this book, but I think that the month of December and possibly January would be the prime time to fish this part of the Fraser River drainage. The main Fraser River is nearly too big to fish for average anglers like myself. I've taken a few fish from it, but the Fraser, like the Columbia River, actually overpowers the imagination of most of us who've tried to fish it at all.

I've had to pass up more rivers and river systems than I've brushed on here. It would take several volumes to give even a fair listing of the streams available in British Columbia. I feel that it will be several years before the American angler will be much bothered by the numbers of anglers he sees on these Canadian streams, and the rivers and creeks mentioned are enough to keep us all busy for some time to come.

Alaska

The problems faced by the steelhead fisherman who wants to take steelheads in Alaskan waters are the same as for the bulk of the British Columbian waters. If anything, the logistics involved in fishing Alaskan waters are far more complex for the angler who is trying to take steelheads during a limited stay. It costs a lot of money to either fish or hunt in Alaska. A guide is almost always essential because the waters of Alaska are so remote from civilization. By the same token, nearly every one of the thousands of streams will have a good run of steelheads in them any time after August or September. And Alaskans think nothing of hopping into the family airplane and flying a few hundred miles to hunt or fish any of these streams.

For instance, Bristol Bay to the north of the Alaskan peninsula has literally hundreds of streams flowing into it. To reach Bristol Bay waters the angler would probably contact a bush pilot in Anchorage and fly in to any recommended waters. The NAKNEK RIVER, ALAGNAK RIVER, MULCHATNA RIVER and any of a hundred other streams will have fish in them during the month of September. So your only problem is to get to them in the first place.

The top month for fishing steelheads in Alaskan waters is either late October or November. And about the only time there will be a scarcity of fish is mid-summer from late June until late July. KETCHICAN CREEK, WARD CREEK can be fished from Ketchican. Air service will get you into the NAHA RIVER, THORNE RIVER, KARTA RIVER, as well as LAKE MCDONALD OUTLET, FISH CREEK, and KLAWAK CREEK. All you've got to do is bring your own sleeping bag and plenty of fishing gear. But the problem is still getting to the streams and not catching steelheads once they are reached.

Who to Contact—British Columbia

CAMPBELL RIVER AND OYSTER RIVER   ISLAND
Saratoga Beach Resort; RR1, Campbell River
The Breakers Resort; RR1, Campbell River
Silver Sands Beach Resort; RR1, Campbell River
Don Marshall; Box 62, Campbell River (guide)
David Williamson, RR1, Campbell River (guide)

COURTENAY
Clifton Motel; Box 1423, Ph: 55
El Morocco Motel; 155 17th St., Ph: 1245
River View Motel; P. O. Box 419, Ph: 1476L

DUNCAN
Commercial Hotel; Ph: 1760
Riverside Auto Court & Trailer Park; RR3, Ph: Duncan 686
Tzouhalem Hotel; Box 514

LAKE COWICHAN
Blome's Lakeside Resort
Cedar Resort
Sunset Auto Park; Box 349
Arthur Hancock; (guide)

NANAIMO
Balmoral Hotel; 126 Haliburton St., Ph: SK 4-4714
Bluebird Motel; 995 Terminal Ave., Ph: SK 4-6541
Tallo-Ho Travelodge; 1 Terminal Ave., Ph: SK 3-2241

PORT ALBERNI
Alberni's Motel; 109 Rogers St., Ph: 723-9072
Hotel Barclay Ltd., 720 Third Avenue
Sunset Motel & Trailer Park; 1615 McIntyre Dr., Ph: 723-2231

QUALICUM BEACH
Crescent Motel; Ph: SK 2-2491
Eaglecrest Lodge
Sunset Inn Ltd.
Freeman Russell, RR1 (guide)
Thomas Walker, RR1 (guide)

SAYWARD
Salmon River Hotel
White River Court, Island Highway Ph: KB524

VICTORIA
Colony Motor Hotel; 2852 Douglas St.
Firwood Lodge; 905 Cook St.
Surf Hotel; 290 Dallas Rd., Ph: EV 6-3305
George Robertson, 2329 Blanshard St., (guide)

BELLA COOLA   MAINLAND
Bella Coola Lodge
Talchako Lodge; Box 47

Tweedsmuir Lodge
Gordon Corbould (guide)
G. A. Elsey (guide)
Clayton Mack (guide)

HOPE
Lyn-Al Motel; Box 372, Ph: UN 6-3326
Riviera Motel; Box 817, Ph: UN 6-5731
Swiss Chalet; Box 308, Ph: UN 6-3456

KAMLOOPS
El Camno Motel; RR2, Ph: 372-8710
Mayfair Motor Court; RR2, Ph: 372-8933
Monte Vista Motel; RR2, Ph: 372-3033
Arthur Beecraft, Box 404 (guide)
Gordon Cahility; 723 Nicola St. (guide)
Douglas Ellis, RR2 (guide)

NEW HAZELTON
New Hazelton Motel
New Hazelton Cabins; Box 68, Ph: 137M
Rainbow Motel; Ph: 52Y
Theodore Campbell; Box 215 Hazelton (guide)
John Lee; Box 213, Hazelton (guide)
Walter Love; Box 211, Hazelton (guide)

PORT MOODY
Port Arm Hotel

POWELL RIVER
Kent's Beach Resort; RR1

SQUAMISH
Garibaldi Motor Hotel; Box 570
Garibaldi Mountain Chalets; Box 136
Marland Motel; Box 44, Ph: HU 5-4435
Marine Hotel

PRINCE RUPERT
Parkside Resort Motel; 2000 11th Ave.
Prince Rupert Hotel
Savoy Hotel; 316 Fifth St.
Lee Cannutt; 1409 1st Overlook (guide)

SPENCES BRIDGE
Acacia Motel
Big Horn Court; Box 98

VANCOUVER

Abbotsford Hotel; 921 West Pender St., Ph: MU 1-4335
Hotel Niagra; 435 West Pender St.
Vancouver Travelodge; 1304 Howe St., Ph: MU 2-2767
Henry Delmonico; 1475 Trimble St., (guide)

MISCELLANEOUS

British Columbia Travel Bureau, Dept. of Recreation & Conservation Parliament Buildings, Victoria, B.C.
Canadian Government Travel Bureau, Ottawa
Department of Recreation & Conservation; Fish and Game Branch, 525 Fort St., Victoria, B.C.
Director, Pacific Area, Dept. of Fisheries, 1155 Robson Street, Vancouver, B.C.
Greater Vancouver Visitors and Convention Bureau, 596 W. Georgia St. Vancouver 2, B.C.
Texaco Touring Bureau, 501 Graphic Arts Building; 1200 W. Pender St., Vancouver, B.C.
The Victoria & Island Publicity Bureau, 786 Government St., Victoria, B.C.

Tourist Information Centers:
Terminal Ave., Nanaimo
McBride St. & 1st Ave., Prince Rupert
363 George St., Prince George
207 Seymour St., Kamloops
Willows Hotel, Campbell River

Who to Contact—Alaska

All listings are guides and air service.

ANCHORAGE

Eldon Brandt; Box 1031
Ben C. White; 1513 F Street
Ken Oldham & Son; Box 3-127
Prince William Sound Guides; P. O. Box 4141
J. Stubbins; 6006 De Barr Road
Jeff Brown; 3305 Turnagain Blvd. East
Jack Lee; 5706 Ladd Street

HAINES

Fox Air Service; P. O. Box 95

KENAI

Lewis & Associates; Box 511
Donald L. Johnson; Box 152

KING SALMON
Nickles Floatplane Service; Box 7

KODIAK
Outdoor Guides; P. O. Box 2259
Bill Pinnell

MISCELLANEOUS
Alaska Dept. of Fish and Game; Subport Building, Juneau
Division of Tourism & Economic Development, Juneau

18 Future Steelheads

The future of the steelheads is far brighter than for many other fish species. As long as there is any reasonably clear, clean water flowing into the Pacific Ocean from a creek, river, or brook of even the smallest size, the steelheads will run and spawn.

Even in the virgin days before the white men came to settle the Pacific slope and to pollute its streams and cut down its watersheds, the steelheads were never as numerous as the salmons. This is still the same circumstance to be found in virtually every stream where the two types of fish run. And there is a very specific reason for this.

Most of the salmons run into the same streams as the steelheads. They spawn in roughly the same type of water, and they need the same clean, unpolluted water that the steelheads need. But, most of the important salmon species have one trait that the steelheads lack. They migrate back to salt water sooner than the steelheads. And this is the basic reason that the steelheads were never as numerous.

To most steelhead fishermen it doesn't seem important that the steelhead normally has to stay in fresh water for

two full years or more before he is ready to go back to the
ocean. But this single factor automatically limits the
number of fish that can survive in any stream. And the
amount of water, plus the fertility or carrying capacity of
that water when it is at lowest ebb—normally during the
late summer months—is the gauge of how many steelheads a stream can support. It took the biologists a long
time and a lot of money to discover this simple, basic fact.

During the early thirties when it was obvious that the
steelheads were getting scarce in most streams, the first,
and most logical solution to the problem seemed to be to
take the eggs from the females and the milt from the males
and artificially rear steelheads. The main reason that this
looked like the proper solution was that high dams were
being built in places that blocked the fish from their
natural spawning channels upstream. Also, the lumber
empires that had been carved out of the Pacific forests had
cut deeply into these same spawning beds because the
loosened earth silted down the necessary gravel. So, millions upon millions of steelhead eggs were fertilized, raised
to the fingerling stage, and more or less haphazardly
dumped into the streams. This whole operation netted
no detectable increase in the numbers of returning
spawners in the vast majority of streams. For many more
years fish and game managers tried to improve the fishing
in these streams by just increasing the number of fry that
they planted. These were merely bigger and more expensive failures.

Finally it was determined that any stream would just
support and send so many fish to the ocean. The limiting
factor was the carrying capacity of the streams for those
two critical years, not the number that were successfully
spawned or planted.

The next solution that the biologists tried was to keep

the young steelheads in the hatcheries until they had reached a stage of growth where they were ready to migrate to the ocean. This had an immediate effect on the streams. Today this is the normal method of stocking a steelhead stream. Even today, the *number* of fish actually planted in the coastal streams is rarely as large as the number that were planted in the late thirties. But the total *number* of *pounds* of fish is larger, and the number of successfully returning, mature fish has climbed steadily. This is where the matter seems to be lying at the present time, and where it probably will stay for some time to come.

There is an important reason why the situation probably will not change for a long time in most steelhead fishing areas. Recent research has found that even where the fishing pressure is heaviest, as in California and Oregon, fishermen are not doing very much to cut down the supply of steelheads which ultimately reach the spawning beds and hatcheries. In other words, fishing is not hurting the supply of fish for the future.

Statistically, it has been found that if 10 to 20 per cent of the fish successfully make it past the fishermen to their natural spawning ground, this is sufficient to more than supply the correct number of fish to suit the carrying capacity of that stream. Naturally, the bigger and more fertile the stream is, the more fish it can carry. And if the fish and game men should find that this necessary number of fish have not made it to the natural spawning beds, they could merely inject the correct number of hatchery reared fish and the situation comes back to normal for any given stream. Too, even under the heaviest fishing conditions, the fishermen to date haven't been able to take much more than 50 per cent of the available fish in the rivers, and then only rarely. So, there is a fairly large margin to work with.

So, it would seem there are a lot of steelheads going to waste! I've noticed that whenever the cry goes up that fishing is getting bad, the politician steps in and lowers the limit on a given species. At present, this is the case with steelhead fishing. So, if at least 30 per cent of the available steelheads are not being utilized, and if angling pressure is such a small item in the determination of the worth of a steelhead stream, why hasn't the same politician come up with a liberalized limit? Never, to my knowledge, has the limit ever been raised on any trout or salmon species!!!

When I have talked to game managers and biologists about these things, they merely shrug and point out that the fishing population for steelheads is increasing every year. In fact, the angling population, at the present time, is increasing at the rate of 20 per cent a year, so if they go on at this rate, they will double every five years. And the fisheries' managers and biologists are afraid to go to bat for a bigger limit. Anyway, to most sportsmen, two or three steelheads in a day is plenty. And there is far more important work that the biologists could be doing.

Probably the future of steelheading, as well as that of most fish or game species, lies in the realm of the scientific breakthrough. In this day and age of the atom it is astounding that more attention isn't paid to the men who know what thay are doing: the specialist, the fisheries' biologist, and the icthyologist. These men know what is necessary, but they are so hamstrung by sentimental sportsmen and by ignorant politicians that they are either afraid to speak up, or they simply no longer care.

In the case of the steelheads alone, there are several

directions in which most biologists would like to go. And the odd thing about the situation is that most of the basic, scientific knowledge is already in their possession. From the fisherman's point of view, he merely wants to have more fish to angle for, in spite of the statistics which show, apparently, that he is not taking enough of the fish that are already there. And the biologist wants to utilize the fisheries. So, is there any way out of this dilemma?

At the present time, there is still the big bottleneck of the carrying capacity of the steelhead streams to deal with whenever the biologist tries to do something about managing a steelhead stream fishery. It would be a simple matter for them to merely double the hatchery output and keep dumping more and more migration-sized fish into the streams. This automatically would tend to increase the number of returning steelheads from the ocean. And this is what the "get more fish quickly" politicians and fishermen are forcing the biologist and fisheries managers to do. It is a very expensive way to go about the job, and it is still limited by the nature of the streams and the nature of the fish themselves. However, there are some promising ideas that the scientists have been dabbling with for several years.

A fisheries' biologist, icthyologist or fisheries' manager will instantly refuse to make any kind of definite statement on just about any subject if he has even the vaguest hint that the statements might get into print in any form. It has been the experience of every one of them, that everytime they are quoted, no matter what the subject, the angling population instantly chooses up sides. The politicians then keep their ear tuned to find out which side has the most votes, and the scientific man ends up right in the middle of an argument, which at best was probably just a theory on his part in the first place. But in private, I have managed to buttonhole several of these men and have asked them what the problems *probably* are in steelhead fishing. They opened up only slightly, and then only after an iron guarantee that they would not be directly quoted.

The basic problem is to get the steelheads to migrate downstream as quickly as possible after spawning. There is a good possibility that this could be done by selective breeding. A good example of what can be done with selective breeding is the work of Dr. Lauren Donaldson of the School of Fisheries at the University of Washington. (Not one of the men to whom I have talked.) Dr. Donaldson was trying to selectively breed rainbow trout, and he succeeded in a big way. He started with wild fish which were producing approximately 1000 eggs per female at the end of four years and ended up with two year old females that were producing an average of 10,000 eggs at the end of their second year. These fish were reaching the astounding size of 3 to 5 lbs. at the end of one year and 7 to 14 lbs. at the end of the second year. This has to be measured against the average 6 to 9 in. fish that are naturally produced in a steelhead stream in the same two year period. Too, there is probably no limit as to how far this experiment could be carried, if there was a reason to go on with it.

Another example of what the scientists can do when they are given a little leeway is a California experiment carried on at the Hot Creek Hatchery, where the biologists convinced the rainbows that they should spawn in the fall instead of the normal spawning date during the spring months.

Now, just working with these two examples, there are several directions in which the scientists can go. First of all, would the super trout from Dr. Donaldson's ponds still show the same growing characteristics if they were merely dropped in a nearby stream and allowed to fend for themselves? Probably not, because any fish species will control his own size to suit the carrying capacity of the stream or body of water in which he lives. Could these fish be induced, as the Hot Creek trout were, to spawn in the fall as well as spring? They probably could.

The fish Dr. Donaldson is raising obviously can't be kept in a hatchery for two years on a large scale. It would be kind of pointless to release trout that were from 7 to 14 lbs., and they would probably bankrupt any fish and game department that tried to raise them because they are such big eaters. There is still that item of getting the fish to migrate to salt water where the food supply is virtually unlimited.

The logical approach would seem to be to get the scientist to work on breeding Dr. Donaldson's type of super fish, then to make them migrate at different times of the year, and above all, to get them to move out of the streams as soon as possible. If the scientists only managed to create a strain of steelheads that would migrate during their first year, they could almost guarantee that the carrying capacity of the streams would be automatically doubled. It would actually be more than doubled because the small steelheads eat far more during their second year than they do during the first year in the stream.

When I asked if the fish could be bred to migrate to the ocean sooner, most of the biologists stated that it shouldn't be too difficult to accomplish. But none of them knew of any attempts to accomplish it. When I asked if they could be bred to spawn at different times of the year, such as summer and fall, they stated that this had already been done. But they all pointed out that it wouldn't make much sense to get the fish into the streams during the summer months because streams were too low and warm at that time of the year. They also pointed out that it would do no good until the fish were induced to leave the streams immediately, and that there would probably be complications because they would also have to breed fish that could stand higher water temperatures. What was wrong with this, I asked? Could it be done? Yes, was the answer, but what would this do to the sea life of the steelheads? They might change their pattern of existence in the ocean and cause some kind of upheaval in the life pattern of other species; perhaps the salmons, which liked the warmer, surface waters of the oceans.

The next item of interest to the angler is the matter of artificial spawning channels. With salmon in British Columbia, Washington, and California, it has been proved that these fish can and will breed in man-made gravel beds. What they have done is to prepare an area right next to the regular stream bed and then to flood it with stream water. There are many thousands of miles of streams suitable for this kind of operation, because the majority of any stream is made up of water that does not measure up to that required by fish for spawning, such as deep, slow pools and steep riffles. This is the probable direction of the future salmon spawning areas. In the case of the salmons it makes sense because these fish are of primary interest to the angler and the commercial fisherman while they are still in the ocean or in the tidal stretches of most streams. But it would still not make sense for the steelheads because, unlike the salmons, the steelheads still would have to remain in the streams for that fateful two years.

The state of Washington is even pushing the idea of "Fish Farms" where salmons are artificially spawned close to the ocean, so we can expect some big things from this type of experimentation. In the past the salmon has always had a bigger voice in the fishing world because he is important to the sportsman, but also to the commercial fisherman, who traditionally has a lot to say about everything through their tightly organized group approach to the subject. And the reason that they are pressing for some solution to the problem of the spawning beds of the salmons is that these fish (as well as the steelheads) are being cut off from their natural waters by high dams in ever increasing numbers throughout the entire range of both fish. But where does this leave the steelhead who needs the same kind of support?

The way I see the thing, it is absolutely necessary for the scientists to solve the problem of getting the steelheads back to the ocean as soon as possible after they spawn. The tiny migrants that go down to the ocean at 6 to 9 in. are of little use to anyone, and the economics of catching a steelhead has proven that the necessary cost of solving this problem is worthwhile. In a recent California survey it was learned that a hatchery stocked steelhead cost over $8.00 for the fish and game department to provide. But the survey also showed that it cost the angler $40 to catch that same steelhead. This is a 500 per cent profit; pretty good economics anyway you look at the thing. Just taking moderate statistics, if a million steelheads are caught every year, we are dealing with a forty-million dollar industry! And of this amount, about thirty-two million dollars goes into someone's pocket.

There are many unanswered questions about steelheads. Where do they go when they are in the ocean? What is the mortality rate in the ocean as compared to the stream mortality? Is there any problem of hybrid species dominating the natural strains that have weathered the hard school of time? Does it make sense to try to utilize the streams during the entire year? Is there any way to increase the carrying capacity of individual streams? And these are only a few . . .

Habitat improvement about which we hear so much is a creeping thing throughout the range of the steelheads. Poor lumbering practices ruin more good water each year than the stream clearance programs manage to give back to the fish. Gravel removal for construction takes even bigger bites in the spawning beds of the steelhead and the salmons. Bigger and bigger dams are going up at a faster rate every year. And it is very probable that there will never be a solution to the problem of how to get the fish over these barriers, let alone get the downstream fish back to the ocean again. The steelheads' future is shrinking every season, and the only solution I can see is some kind of scientific help. I have never seen the welfare of fish put before that of the business man, the farmer, or the lumber baron.

At the present time the increased use of chemical fertilizers and pesticides is the biggest threat to the future of the steelheads, as well as the salmons in most areas. But it is also very doubtful that any group of fishermen or any legislature will be able to cut down the amount of these chemicals which the farmer will ultimately use. Every time there is a dam built, for instance, the steelhead fishermen have more or less banded together to fight for the rights of the fish. The best they have been able to do is to force the dam builders to provide for the future of the fish by establishing some sort of hatchery that can replace the estimated number of fish that are lost to the spawning beds blocked off by the dam. And chemical farming is a far more decentralized menace than any dam which can be looked at with the naked eye.

The most logical solution to improved fishing for the

future would be some kind of board of trustees, on the order of the commission system that is now in effect in most states and in Canada. But the big necessity is that this board should be made up of men who know the intricacies of fish and game management and are relatively free from political interference, as the present commissioners are not. It seems almost impossible to consider that a commissioner who perhaps owns a boot factory or a resort could possibly know what is required to manage the fishing or hunting in a large area. And to top off the ridiculousness of the thing, most of these commissioners work only part time at their jobs, regardless of how dedicated they are.

If a board of trained scientists had the authority to manage the fish and game policies *for the benefit of the fish and game,* the problems would be solved much more quickly and cheaply than the current method of juggling statistics against the desires of several million miscellaneous sportsmen. This authority would have to extend right down to opening and closing seasons and would absolutely have to include the power to embark on new lines of research, even if they will not bear fruit for a long time.

The steelheads are in pretty fair shape at present, but the things that have been done to keep them from being eliminated are scientific, such as the stocking of migrant-sized fish, the potentials of selectively breeding for disease resistance and increased fertility. The political management of these fisheries, as well as most other fish or game management, has never, to my knowledge, produced anything of lasting value to sportsmen.

But how one goes about letting the men who know what they are doing and know what is necessary do what they should is an insoluble problem at the present time.

It is fairly obvious that sooner or later the angling population will force the necessary changes onto the politicians
who control the fisheries' managers. In California alone
there are already over fifteen million citizens and over
10 per cent of them are fishermen who have voting
rights. This will certainly cause some kind of change in
the slowly declining yield of our sporting species. And
when the need arises for a change I have no doubt that
it will come. It's unfortunate that the change can't be
made before the situation gets desperate.

Index